THE
BERLIN 1945 BATTLEFIELD GUIDE

THE BERLIN 1945 BATTLEFIELD GUIDE

PART 1

THE BATTLE OF THE ODER-NEISSE

DAVID McCORMACK

FONTHILL

*To my good friends on both sides of the pond,
whose support is greatly valued*

Fonthill Media Language Policy

Fonthill Media publishes in the international English language market. One language edition is published worldwide. As there are minor differences in spelling and presentation, especially with regard to American English and British English, a policy is necessary to define which form of English to use. The Fonthill Policy is to use the form of English native to the author. David McCormack was born and educated in Bolton, Lancashire and therefore British English has been adopted in this publication.

Fonthill Media Limited
Fonthill Media LLC
www.fonthillmedia.com
office@fonthillmedia.com

First published in the United Kingdom and the United States of America 2017

British Library Cataloguing in Publication Data:
A catalogue record for this book is available from the British Library

ISBN 978-1-78155-607-8

Typeset in 10pt on 13pt Sabon
Printed and bound by CPI Group (UK) Ltd, Croydon, CR0 4YY

Acknowledgements

My heartfelt thanks to Tim Cockitt for his sterling work as my proofreader. Also, I must thank the alumni and Advancement Services at the University of Salford for their continued support. My everlasting gratitude goes out to author and friend Linda Stratmann, whose infectious energy and creativity spurred me on to complete my first book, which was released in 2016. Special recognition goes to Jenny Young, whose warmth, understanding, and unstinting support has been inspirational.

CONTENTS

1

Exploring the Oder-Neisse Battlefields

The purpose of this guide is to encourage and assist people in visiting the battlefields on the direct approaches to Berlin, which were the scenes of fierce combat in April 1945. There are, of course, various organised tours run by a series of long established battlefield tour operators, such as Leger Battlefield Tours and Stephen Ambrose Historical Tours (for American visitors). These tours usually last between seven and twelve days, and provide an excellent introduction for those keen to know more about military history, or those who are visiting a battlefield for the first time. For single travellers, there is the advantage of being part of a group that shares a similar interest, added to which, there is the possibility of socialising in the evenings. Tour operators take the strain off passengers who may be unfamiliar with foreign travel, or those who simply wish to have an 'all inclusive' experience in which transfers, accommodation, and guided excursions are part of an overall package.

While organised tours generally provide a value-for-money experience, they are not necessarily the best option for the more seasoned traveller, who may feel constrained by tight itineraries that leave limited time slots to see individual viewpoints on the battlefield. Also, those with more in-depth knowledge of the subject can sometimes feel a little frustrated by the delivery of the guide or speaker who is obliged to cater for a wide audience. Travelling independently removes many of the time constraints imposed by organised tours, as you essentially become your own tour manager. This of course takes a certain degree of confidence, and not a little effort. This guidebook will make the process of organising and conducting your own tour of the Oder-Neisse battlefields less stressful, and therefore, more satisfying.

Travelling independently can of course raise a few practical issues. Long periods of driving require more than one person to take their turn at the wheel. Furthermore, actually getting to your desired location can also present problems. While 'satnav' addresses have been provided for every viewpoint, experience shows that it is always wise to back up the device with a good map. If you plan to make extensive use of your satnav, it would be a good idea to ensure that the latest map updates have been installed. In addition to navigation aids, a mobile phone is an essential piece of kit. It is advisable to have the numbers for your hotel, car hire, and local emergency services stored in your phone before you set off on your battlefield adventure.

Visiting battlefields is a hugely worthwhile experience in that it brings the history to life. There is simply nothing to compare with being at the very site of a particular action, to literally walk in the footsteps of heroes (or in some cases villains). The author has visited battlefield sites for over thirty years and has worked as a battlefield guide since 2012. As such, he can attest to the value in visiting battlefields, either as part of an organised tour, or as an independent traveller. Above all, no matter how you choose to travel, enjoy yourself.

How the Guide is Laid Out

This guide is aimed at both novice and more experienced battlefield enthusiasts. Prior knowledge is not assumed. Therefore, there are a number of chapters devoted wholly to the historical background of planning and subsequent operations along the direct approaches to Berlin. The operations of both German Army Group Vistula and the two main Red Army Fronts, which confronted it are given equal weighting. Essentially, the guide follows the chronology of the last desperate battles along the approaches to Berlin. The six one-day tours included in the guide begin with the first crossings of the Oder in January 1945. They end with the tightening of the noose around Berlin four months later. These tours can be undertaken individually, or as part of much wider exploration of the Oder-Neisse battlefields. All tours are essentially circular and include suggestions for lunch breaks along the way. If you intend to complete all six of the tours, you will need to allocate between eight to ten days, depending on whether your mode of travel towards Berlin is via passenger aircraft or motor transport.

Visiting the Oder-Neisse Battlefields

If you are planning to fly to Berlin and then rent a car, there are currently two operating airports, Tegel and Schonefeld. A third airport, Berlin Brandenburg, was due to open in the second half of 2017. However, numerous delays have seen the new airport's completion and opening put back several times. In the meantime, more investment has been put into the existing airports in an effort to cope with rising passenger numbers.

Car hire is fairly simple as there are a number of firms to choose from, including Avis, Europcar, and Enterprise Rent-A-Car. If you are planning to take your own car, there is the option of either taking the ferry or Eurotunnel. There are plenty of advantages in using your own transport, but it will significantly increase your driving time. It is also advisable to look at the websites of the AA and RAC as part of your tour preparation, as both provide good advice regarding driving in Europe.

The author recommends Berlin as your tour base as there is a wide variety of accommodation to choose from. The six tours included in this guide all have Berlin as their starting point. However, if you choose to stay elsewhere, such as in Seelow or Frankfurt-an-der-Oder, you can simply adjust the tour instructions to suit your needs. An early start (8 a.m.–8.30 a.m.) is advised as time and place always involves compromises, particularly if you are tempted to visit sites that lure you away from your planned itinerary. This guide is all about making your visit to the battlefields easier. It is in no way prescriptive. At any time, you can deviate from the suggested tour routes. It is your adventure.

Recommended Maps

For the Seelow, Reitwein, and Frankfurt-an-der-Oder area, the author recommends the 1:100,000 scale Landkreis Markish-Oderland and the 1:70,000 scale Markische Schweiz Berliner Urstromtal Frankfurt/Oder maps, which are available from Amazon, some German petrol stations, and some tourist information offices.

For the Cottbus area, the author recommends the 1: 70,000 scale Cottbus Lausitzer Seenland, the 1:100,000 scale Radwanderkarte Spree–Neisse–Cottbus, Furst-Puckler region, and the 1:50,000 scale Spremberg und Umgebung maps. For the Schwedt area, the author recommends the 1:100,000 scale Schwedt/Oder map. For the Zossen area, the author recommends the 1:55,000 scale Sudliches Berlin–Teltow, Ludwigsfelde, und Umgebung and the 1:25,000 scale Zossen maps.

It is perhaps a worthwhile idea to purchase maps before setting off, as studying them beforehand will enable you to become more familiar with the ground (all of the above maps can be purchased reasonably cheaply on sites such as Amazon or eBay).

Cycle Routes

Using cycles to explore battlefield areas is becoming increasing popular among both independent travellers and tour companies. Certain sections of the Oder-Neisse battlefields are ideal for cyclists. The terrain along the banks of the Oder and Neisse rivers is mainly asphalted and largely free of traffic. There are also numerous crossing points into Poland along the way.

There are numerous bike rental outlets in and around Berlin. Many of the larger Berlin hotels can also arrange for bike hire. The following websites provide useful information on cycling and bike hire:

www.oderneisse-radweg.de
www.bicyclegermany.com
www.brandenberg-tourism.com/discover-brandenberg/brandenberg-by-bike.html

Suggested Reading

Prior to starting your exploration of the battlefields, the author suggests the following titles for background reading and research:

Anthony Beevor: *Berlin: The Downfall 1945*
Vasili I. Chuikov: *The Fall of Berlin*
John Erickson: *The Road to Berlin*
Ian Kershaw: *Hitler 1936-1945: Nemesis*
Erich Kuby: *The Russians and Berlin: 1945*
Catherine Merridale: *Ivan's War: The Red Army 1939-45*
Richard Overy: *Russia's War*
Geoffrey Roberts: *Stalin's General: The Life of Georgy Zhukov*
Cornelius Ryan: *Berlin 1945: The Last Battle*
William J. Spahr: *Zhukov: The Rise & Fall of a Great Captain*
John Toland: *The Last 100 Days*
Georgy Zhukov: *Marshal of Victory*

Suggested Viewing

The author recommends the following DVDs:

Line of Fire: The Battle of Berlin
The World at War: Nemesis (Germany March–May 1945)
The War of the Century: When Hitler Fought Stalin

2
House of Cards

Received wisdom has it that in military terms, Germany was a spent force by the end of 1944. Certainly, this fateful year had been one of unmitigated disaster, as defeat followed defeat, followed by impending defeat. On land, fighting a multi-front war had cost Germany 106 divisions (destroyed or disbanded) between 1 June and 30 November 1944. At sea, the command of the ocean had long since passed to the Allies. In the air, massive bomber fleets continued to lay waste to both industry and housing stocks.

Hitler was at first slow to respond to the changing fortunes of war. However, in September 1944, he finally gave his support to the total war policies advocated since Stalingrad by Minister of Public Enlightenment and Propaganda, Joseph Goebbels. The subsequent mass mobilisation of manpower revived Germany's waning combat power, making it possible to scrape together a strategic reserve of men and machines. As the year drew towards its close, this build-up of German combat power led to Hitler's views concerning the overall strategic picture becoming more sanguine.

His optimism was not totally unfounded. In the west, the Allied advance had bogged down in the wake of the doomed Market Garden operation. Indeed, all Montgomery had to show for his grand scheme was a huge casualty list and the occupation of a salient, which in reality was nothing more than a strategic cul-de-sac. For the time being at least, the initiative had been wrested from the Allies. On the Eastern Front, Operation Bagration had finally succumbed to the law of diminishing returns as the Red Army's massive westwards thrust ran out of steam on the banks of the Vistula. The wide ranging operations conducted by the Red Army in the summer of 1944 had served to finally liberate Mother Russia and create favourable jumping off points in Poland for the next great strategic leap. However, losses had been heavy, and the Red Army's tenuous supply chain was stretched to its absolute limit. It would take several months for the vast Soviet forces to regroup and resupply. This much-needed respite on both main battlefronts opened up strategic avenues for Hitler that inevitably brought about a conflict of ideas with his pugnacious Chief of Staff, General Heinz Guderian.

For Hitler, the accumulation of reserves meant the prospect of major offensive operations and a chance to score a huge military and political success. To this end, 1,378 tanks and self-propelled guns out of a total production figure of 2,299 for the months November–December 1944 were allocated for his planned offensive in the west. On 11 December, he met with his commanders at Ziegenberg to outline his thinking behind this last throw of the dice in the west. The main thrust of his briefing was to stress his view that only an offensive strategy would enable the people to endure further hardships, as it would preserve their faith in the ultimate victory. With these psychological considerations in mind, Hitler said that, 'I have striven from the beginning to conduct the war wherever possible offensively.' He went on to expound his views by stating:

> Wars are finally decided through the recognition by one side or the other that the war as such can no longer be won. To get the enemy to realise this is therefore the most important task ... It is also important to strengthen these psychological factors in letting no moment pass without making plain to the enemy that whatever he does, he can never reckon with capitulation, never, never. That is the decisive point.

General Heinz Guderian. (*Author's collection*)

His optimism was a triumph of his unshakable will. To his commanders, Hitler was, despite the occasional slip-up, the supreme optimist. He had to be, for there was no alternative way out of the catastrophe he had done so much to create.

After several cancellations, the offensive (codenamed 'Autumn Mist') was finally launched on 18 December. After achieving complete tactical surprise, and making some initial gains, the offensive quickly bogged down. On 23 December, Guderian set off on the long drive from Zossen, determined to 'request that the battle, which is causing us heavy casualties, be broken off and that all the forces that could be spared be immediately transferred to the Eastern Front.' He was well briefed for the anticipated confrontation with Hitler. General Reinhard Gehlen's (Chief of Foreign Armies East) carefully prepared intelligence reports indicated that nine Soviet Fronts were gearing up for a massive series of offensives along a battlefront, which extended from Memel in the Baltic, down to the River Drava in southern Hungary. The Soviet forces were by now both massive and very capable. Gehlen believed that they would strike 'towards the middle of January' and that the outcome would inevitably be the total destruction of German land forces in the east.

Despite the Ardennes offensive having failed to achieve the decisive results he wished for, Hitler still believed that he held the initiative on the Western Front. Guderian's arguments in favour of transferring all available forces to the west were dismissed by Hitler as he clung stubbornly to his offensive mantra. Gehlen's estimates of Soviet strength and intentions were ridiculed as being pure fabrication. None of Guderian's arguments moved Hitler, who was so convinced that his strategy in the west was paying dividends, that he ordered a subsidiary operation codenamed 'North Wind' to take the pressure off the 5th Panzer Army in the Ardennes. Guderian went back to his headquarters empty-handed, fulminating about the pig headed 'ostrich strategy' that, in his view, stupidly ignored the massive threat in the east.

On 28 December, Hitler once again addressed his commanders. He enjoined them to fight on, or condemn the German people to enslavement, torture, and death at the hands of a vengeful enemy. There was an admission that a second Dunkirk was no longer possible. However, he claimed that some positive results had been achieved from the Ardennes offensive. Did Hitler really believe that the war could still be prosecuted to a successful conclusion guaranteeing the continued existence of the Reich? Or was his address merely a sham performance designed to instil hope in those whose sound military judgement had already led them to conclude that all was lost? The text of the briefing is quoted *in extensio* so that Hitler's decision to ignore Guderian's warnings concerning the threat in the east can be contextualised:

> Gentlemen. I have asked you to come here before an operation on the successful conclusion of which further blows in the west will depend. First, I

want briefly to place this particular operation in its true significance. I want to relate it to the overall situation that confronts us, and to the problems which we face and which must be solved. Whether they develop in a happy or an unhappy fashion, solved they shall be, ending either in our favour or in our destruction. The German situation can be characterised in a few sentences. As in the Great War, so in this war the question is not whether Germany will be graciously permitted by her enemies, in the event of their victory, some kind of existence, but whether Germany has the will to remain in existence or whether it will be destroyed.

Unlike earlier wars of the seventeenth or eighteenth century, this war will decide neither a question of political organisation nor a question of the adherence of a folk or tribe or a former federal state to the German Reich. What, in the final analysis, will be decided is the survival of the very essence of our German folk, not survival of the German Reich. A victory by our enemies must bolshevise Europe. What bolshevisation means for Germany everybody must and will realise ... Preservation is our goal. The destruction of the essence under certain circumstances destroys the race forever. Struggles such as are going on now have the character of clashes of world views. Therefore they are not comparable to the struggles of the time of Frederick the Great ... The German Reich is now fighting an ideological war for its very existence... The loss of this war will destroy the German folk and break it up ... I hasten to add, gentlemen, that from these statements of mine you are not to draw the conclusion that I even remotely envisage the loss of the war. In my life I have never learned to know the word capitulation... I mention this only because I want you to understand why I pursue my aim with such fanaticism, and why nothing can wear me down. As much as I may be tormented with worries, and even physically shaken by them, nothing will make the slightest change in my decision to fight on until at last the scales tip on our side.

In a military sense it is decisive that in the west we are moving from a sterile defensive to the offensive. The offensive alone will enable us to give once more to this war in the west a successful turn ... The view that under all circumstances an offensive would be more costly in blood than a defensive is wrong ... If we take into account the losses of the enemy and our own losses, and if we include the number of war prisoners, offensive battles have always been favourable to us ... Although, unfortunately, the offensive has not resulted in the decisive success which might have been expected, yet a tremendous easing of the situation has occurred. The enemy has had to abandon all his plans for attack ... His operational plans have been completely upset ... Already he has to admit that there is no chance of the war being decided before August, perhaps not before the end of next year ...

Our firm aim must be to clear up the situation in the west by offensive action. We must be fanatical in this aim... How important it is to get an early

> decision you will realise from the following. The enemy has full knowledge of the flying bombs and has reconstructed them entirely ... Everything, therefore, speaks in favour of cleaning up this situation before the enemy begins to use superweapons of this kind.
>
> The German folk have breathed more freely during recent days. We must prevent this relief from being followed by lethargy—lethargy is the wrong word, I mean resignation ... Nothing will deter the nation—whether I order a new textile collection, or some other collection, or whether I call for men. The youth will come forward enthusiastically. The German folk as a whole will react in a thoroughly positive manner... Finally, I wish to appeal to you to support this operation with all your fire, with all your zest, and with all your energy. This also is a decisive operation ... We shall yet master fate.

Fine words, but they represented the same old tune, in that his unshakable will to fight on was all that mattered. This triumph of hope over sound military logic would eventually push the German people into the abyss.

The attack was launched on New Year's Day and coincided with a major Luftwaffe operation codenamed 'Baseplate.' The three German Corps launched against the overstretched US 7th Army advanced 20 kilometres, threatening Strasbourg. Meanwhile, in the east, Guderian visited the headquarters of Army Group South and Army Group 'A'; what he saw deeply troubled him. The operation to relieve Budapest was running behind schedule and both army groups were expecting to be attacked by numerically superior Soviet forces at any time. Armed with this latest intelligence, Guderian once again set off to try and convince Hitler of the great threat materialising on the Eastern Front. Standing on Hitler's left, Guderian began his report:

> *Mein Führer*. I have come once more again to confer with you in person. We have information that makes it certain that the Russian winter offensive, aimed at Berlin, will begin three days from today, on 12 January. I want to inform you once more, as I did on 24 December and again on 31 December, of the real situation on the Eastern Front. I have brought along General Gehlen to show you any document you may wish to see. On 6 January, I paid a personal visit to Army Group A in Krakow and informed myself of the situation in the sector. Sir, this is the last moment for action. I hope that our report will prompt you to transfer to the eastern front the reinforcements that are needed there—and do it tonight.

Gehlen's reports were dismissed as being 'completely idiotic.' Hitler simply could not believe that Stalin disposed of the enormous forces outlined in Gehlen's reports, arguing that the Red Army relied on 'scraped-up Russian scum' and 'cast-off trash picked up along the way.' He then shouted that the person responsible for producing the reports should be placed in an asylum for the insane. Guderian replied that as he too supported Gehlen's estimates, he should also be placed in the same asylum.

Having rejected all of Guderian's proposals, Hitler then attempted to soothe his ruffled feathers by saying that, 'The Eastern Front has never before possessed such a strong reserve as now. That is your doing. I thank you for it.' Guderian was in no mood to be mollified. Hitler's attempt to charm him was rejected with the cutting retort, 'The Eastern Front is like a house of cards. If the front is broken through at one point all the rest will collapse.' The following morning, the commander of Army Group 'A', General Josef Harpe was informed of the outcome of the military conference by General Wolf-Dietrich von Xylander, who said:

> Army High Command just sent through the results of General Guderian's conference at *Führer* Headquarters. The *Führer* has refused everything: Courland, forces from the west, 'Sleigh Ride'—everything. The front stays where it is. And the situation stays as it is. The *Führer* does not believe there will be a Russian offensive.

Following his return to Zossen, Guderian received fresh information that the Soviet offensive was imminent. Red Army sappers were busy clearing minefields ahead of the bridgeheads, which were increasingly being swollen by the arrival of additional men and materiel. Guderian was now convinced that the offensive was only hours away. Time was fast running out for Hitler's house of cards.

The offensive, which until recently had been dismissed as the fevered ramblings of a madman, materialised in all its terrifying intensity on 12 January. Hitler, whose attention had been consumed by the 'North Wind' operation, finally turned his gaze to the east three days after the Soviet offensive had destroyed the undermanned German defences. Guderian outlined the deteriorating situation in a High Command report dated 15 January:

> *Mein Führer*. I report to you that the situation with Army Group A has worsened. The enemy forces that penetrated from the Baranow bridgehead have, according to the reports we have so far, reached the A-2 position on the general line of Slomniki-Szcekecin west of Wloszczowa and it is predicted they will break through our weak defences there today going towards Krakow and the general line from Kattowitz to Tschenstochau. Although the two divisions that have started to arrive today will delay the enemy thrust towards Upper Silesia between Krakow and Tschenstochau, they will not be able to hold on for a long time at all. The danger for the Upper Silesian industrial region is thus front and centre.

Guderian went on to outline the twin threats emerging from the Radom area and the Pilica. It is interesting to note that it was he, not Hitler, who ordered the transfer of the powerful Panzerkorps Großdeutschland from East Prussia to Łódz. Guderian's role in the transfer of this unit is made explicit in the following section of the report:

> Holding the Pilica front and maintaining the solidarity between the 4th Panzer Army and the 9th Army is particularly important because that is the only way that it will be possible to maintain the conditions under which we can perform countermeasures against the enemy forces operating in the big bend of the Vistula. I have therefore decided to assign the Panzerkorps Großdeutschland, Panzer Grenadier Division *Brandenburg* and the 1st Parachute Division *Hermann Goring*, which is currently en route, to clean up the enemy penetration on the northern bank of the Pilica and then to attack south across the Pilica ... I ask you my *Führer*, to authorise my decision concerning the use of the Panzerkorps Großdeutschland. The overall situation in the middle of the Eastern Front will not be decisively improved through the use of the Panzerkorps Großdeutschland that has been reported or by the infantry divisions coming in to defend the Upper Silesian industrial region. The major Soviet offensive from the great bend in the Vistula that seeks a solution can only be brought to a standstill if additional strong armoured and infantry units are immediately brought to Army Group 'A'.

The substantial reinforcements requested by Guderian never arrived. That evening, Hitler left his headquarters at Ziegenberg for what was to be his final seat of command in Berlin. With the offensive in the west having bogged down, Hitler at last focused his attention on the east. He saw the oil producing areas of Hungary as being more vital to Germany's survival than the coal mines of Silesia. Much to Guderian's chagrin, he transferred the 6th SS Panzer Army to Hungary in a vain attempt to secure the oilfields. However, no matter how many times he shuffled his much reduced deck, events were fast overtaking him. Three days after his return to the capital, Soviet units crossed the 1938 Polish–Silesian frontier to the south of Breslau. The house of cards was collapsing fast.

3

Stalin Takes the Helm

Hitler once said of the Soviet Union, 'you have to kick in the door and the whole rotten structure will come crashing down.' On 22 June 1941, he kicked in the door, and the structure came close to crashing down. However, it did not collapse entirely. Indeed, the survival of the Soviet Union astonished the world. Nevertheless, it could have all ended very differently if the Wehrmacht had been able to fully exploit the Red Army's lack of tactical flexibility. Stalin's heavy-handed approach to operations was no match for the swift encircling manoeuvres executed with great dash and skill by German commanders. His tactics of mounting a forward defence invited disaster. Having suffered defeat after defeat, Stalin acknowledged that the Soviet Union's very survival was at stake. He also recognised his own limitations as a military strategist, all the while remaining conscious of the fate of Tsar Nicholas II, whose self-appointment as Commander in Chief of the Imperial Russian Army led ultimately to his downfall. For Stalin, his priorities were clear, as securing his own position always took precedence over threats to the state.

On 27 August 1942, Stalin appointed Marshal Georgy Zhukov as Deputy Supreme Commander. This appointment was made at a time of crisis, with strong German forces of Army Group 'B' having reached the Volga north of Stalingrad. Further south in the Caucasus region, the 1st Panzer Army was also threatening the oilfields at Grozny. Such a crisis led Stalin to concede that in future, the High Command (*Stavka*) would need to play a more prominent role in formulating strategy. Furthermore, he introduced a collegiate atmosphere in which differences in opinion would be tolerated. Despite the balance of responsibility for operations having tipped in favour of military professionals, Zhukov still had his work cut out as Stalin's naïve take on operational matters had to be managed effectively and its damaging influence limited.

Despite Stalin's acceptance of the new balance of power, the wartime authority of the *Stavka* developed slowly, Chief of Staff Aleksandr Vasilevsky recalled the difficulties the new system experienced in establishing itself: 'Before becoming an effective organ of the Supreme Command, it travelled a path in search of its place in the strategic leadership, its organisational structure, and its methods of work.'

This path became more easily to navigate as the Wehrmacht overstretched itself in the vast hinterland of the Soviet Union in the summer and autumn of 1942. Opportunities arose for the Red Army to first hold, and then go on the offensive by undertaking wide ranging operations deep into the enemy's rear. It was within this new operational environment that the *Stavka* plan to cut off German forces at Stalingrad was created. Zhukov had to skilfully rein in Stalin's aggressive instincts, which would have led to the premature launch of offensive operations. Following the success of Operation Uranus, Stalin's confidence in the military leadership grew and as such the *Stavka* then took on an increasing role in the planning and implementation of operations.

When Stalin surveyed the outcome of the offensive operations conducted by the Red Army between June and October 1944, he did so with some satisfaction. The reforms introduced in the Army and Air Force back in the bleak days of 1942 were bearing fruit as operations conducted on the operational-strategic scale were executed with skill and confidence. All of the political and military objectives set out by the *Stavka* had been achieved and even surpassed. German forces had been ejected from Soviet territory, apart from the Courland Pocket in which Army Group North was hemmed in by General Ivan Bagramyan's 1st Baltic Front. Finland was effectively out of the war following the signing of an armistice on 19 September 1944. In East Prussia, a series of see-saw battles resulted in General Ivan Chernyakhovsky's 3rd Belorussian Front penetrating German territory as far as a line running from Goldap to Augustow. To the south, the Soviet 1st Belorussian, the 2nd Belorussian, and the 1st Ukranian Fronts established bridgeheads on the Narew and the Vistula rivers at Serock, Magnuszew, Pulawy, and Sandomierz. In the Balkans, Marshal Fyodor Tolbukhin's 3rd Ukranian Front and Marshal Rodion Malinovsky's 2nd Ukranian Front cleared Romania and pushed on into Hungary. By the end of 1944, Soviet forces were well placed to move into Austria, bring their operations in Poland and Hungary to a successful conclusion and then push on into Germany, to the very lair of the 'Fascist Beast', Berlin.

The bulk of Soviet forces were positioned in the north between the Niemen and the Gulf of Finland. To the south lay the most direct route into Germany between the Niemen and the Carpathians. The main forces in this area had sat astride the Vistula since August 1944, when a combination of logistical overstretch and fierce German counter-attacks brought Operation Bagration to a halt on the approaches to Warsaw. Casualties had been particularly heavy in operations conducted between Modlin and Praga by the 47th Army, and around Serock and Pultusk by the 70th Army. In September, an attempt to force a crossing of the Vistula by the 1st Polish Army near Praga resulted in further heavy casualties. Acting in his role of *Stavka* representative, Zhukov contacted Stalin to request a halt to all offensive operations in order to reorganise, resupply and reinforce the exhausted forces under his command. Stalin listened to Zhukov's suggestions before replying, 'Fly in with Rokossovsky to General Headquarters tomorrow for a discussion.' There remains some debate as to when the meeting took place as Stalin did not always make a record in his diary. It is most likely that the meeting took place towards the end of October.

The meeting was held in Stalin's office, those also present were General Antonov, Vyacheslav Molotov, Laventry Beria, and Georgy Malenkov. Zhukov spread out his map and began to brief the group on the current situation. Stalin listened to Zhukov's suggestions concerning the adoption of a defensive posture. In his memoirs, Zhukov recalled that his arguments were making a less than favourable impression:

> I saw that Stalin was restless; he would come up to look at the map, then step back, then approach again, eyeing me, the map and Rokossovsky in turn. He even put his pipe aside, which was a sure sign that his composure was slipping and that he was displeased with something.

Stalin persisted in his advocacy of continued offensive operations in the Modlin-Warsaw sector. His obvious displeasure with Zhukov was picked up by Molotov, who in barbed tones said, 'Comrade Zhukov, you are suggesting that the offensive be stopped now that the defeated enemy is unable to stand up to our pressure. Is that sensible?' Stalin then turned to Rokossovsky and asked if he shared Zhukov's opinion. Rokossovsky answered in the affirmative by stating that, 'I believe the troops need a respite to organise themselves after their long and strenuous period of fighting.' Stalin proceeded to undercut Rokossovsky by retorting that, 'the enemy could use a respite to no less advantage than we could.' Shifting his gaze back to Zhukov, Stalin asked for his opinion. Zhukov held his ground, stating:

> My opinion is that this offensive will yield us nothing but casualties. From the operational point of view, we don't particularly need the area northwest of Warsaw. The city must be taken by skirting it to the southwest, and at the same time dealing a powerful cutting blow in the general direction of Łódz-Poznan ... At the same time, the adjacent fronts in the Berlin zone of operations should be thoroughly prepared for joint action.

Stalin interrupted Zhukov to call for a short recess by saying 'go and think over your suggestions some more.' Zhukov and Rokossovsky retired to the library to consider alternative strategies. They were joined fifteen minutes later by Molotov, Beria, and Malenkov. When it became clear that no new ideas had emerged, Stalin reluctantly agreed to halt all offensive operations northwest of Warsaw, though he did so with ill-disguised bad grace. It is quite possible that the outcome of this meeting contributed to Stalin's later decision to abolish the post of Front Coordinator acting on behalf of the Supreme Command.

The key to survival for Stalin's close associates was to gauge his moods. It was quite possible that Zhukov took Stalin's agitation at the meeting as a bad sign and was not entirely surprised when he phoned the following day with the loaded suggestion, 'What would you say to the Stavka taking over control of all fronts in future?' Zhukov took his effective demotion in his stride by replying, 'Yes, there are fewer fronts now ... I think that there is ample opportunity to control the Fronts directly from General Headquarters, since the overall frontage has shrunk, making control of them easier.'

That evening, Stalin informed Zhukov by telephone that he would take over the 1st Belorussian Front from Marshal Rokossovsky, whose forces were currently deployed on the main axis towards Berlin. When Zhukov hesitated out of consideration for Rokossovsky's feelings, Stalin dismissed his concerns by saying, 'We are not pretty maidens.' Zhukov formally assumed command of the 1st Belorussian Front in the 'Berlin Strategic Zone' on 16 November. His relationship with Rokossovsky, who was to take over the command of the 2nd Belorussian Front from Colonel General Georgiy Zakharov was never quite the same again.

It was inevitable that with the end of the war in sight, Stalin would want to re-establish his supreme authority in the conduct of military operations. His main impulse was to enhance his own prestige and begin the process of cutting the military professionals (whom he had relied on so much in times of crisis) back to size. Stalin in effect became his own *Stavka* co-ordinator for the three main fronts involved in the Berlin operation. He had mastered many of the complexities of conducting modern warfare and by this stage of the war felt supremely confident in his own abilities as a war leader. A draft plan that concentrated on the initial phase of the Berlin operation scheduled for January 1945 was worked out by General Antonov, General Sergei Shtemenko, Anotoly Gryzlov, and Nikolai Lomov (officers responsible for planning along specific strategic axes). Stalin reviewed and accepted the plan at the end of November. He was confident that Berlin could be taken in no less than forty-five days, though neither he nor the *Stavka* necessarily equated the capture of Berlin with the end of the war at this stage. It was not only Roosevelt and Eisenhower who had been taken in by the myth of the Alpine Redoubt, as *Stavka* planners also anticipated a spring campaign in southern Germany.

The *Stavka* plan approved by Stalin was a two stage operation with no projected 'operational pause' between phases. The first phase would last for fifteen days, the second thirty. Heavy German resistance was anticipated in East Prussia where Army Group Centre held defences in depth. The difficult task of clearing East Prussia and providing flank protection for the main thrust was entrusted to Rokossovsky's 2nd Belorussian Front and General Ivan Chernyakhovsky's 3rd Belorussian Front. In a separate operation on the southern flank, the 2nd and 3rd Ukranian Fronts closed up between the Tisza and the Danube in December, thereby posing a threat to both Vienna and Budapest, which would draw off German reserves. In the central sector, the two major Army groupings on the Vistula, the 1st Belorussian Front (commanded by Marshal Zukhov) and the 1st Ukrainian Front (commanded by Marshal Konev) were best placed to launch the main offensive aimed at breaking through the German strategic front.

At the Magnuszew bridgehead, Zhukov concentrated Colonel General Vassili Chuikov's 8th Guards Army, Colonel General P. A. Belov's 61st Army, and Lieutenant General N. E. Bezarin's 5th Shock Army for the initial thrust against the German 9th Army. Their main task was to penetrate the German defence to

Joseph Stalin.

a depth of 30 kilometres, thereby opening up their lines for tactical exploitation by Colonel General Mikhail Katukov's 1st Guards Tank Army, Colonel General Semyon Bogdanov's 2nd Guards Tank Army, and Lieutenant General Vladimir Kruikov's 2nd Guards Cavalry Corps. Further south at the Pulawy bridgehead, Zhukov massed Colonel General Vladimir Kolpakchi's 69th Army and Colonel General Viacheslav Tsetaev's 33rd Army. Both of these armies were reinforced with a separate tank corps and their task was to penetrate German defences on a 13-kilometre front, then link up with neighbouring forces to the west, effectively trapping German forces in the process.

At front level, the normal pre-offensive preparations went ahead. In the crucial sector of operations Zhukov had at his disposal a massive force consisting of eight combined-arms armies, two tank armies, two guards cavalry corps, and an air army. Supplying such a concentrated force structure created huge logistical problems. In the second volume of his memoirs, Chuikov recalled the how the challenge of supplying the Front was met:

> Our higher command was in no hurry to begin the decisive advance. We had to build it up in the way needed to assure complete success. There was a mass of construction work to be done, or redone in improved form, on highways, non-metalled roads and on railways. There were tens of thousands of tons of fuel to be brought up, millions of mortar bombs and shells and hundreds of millions of cartridges, and all the equipment and provisions needed to keep us in the field. And all these colossal quantities of stores had to be brought up as close as possible to the front line, to give us the necessary conditions for a breakthrough in depth and the gaining of the scope for manoeuvre.

Preparations for the forthcoming offensive were further complicated by the absence of partisan intelligence and hostile activities that threatened the movement of supplies to a much greater extent than when communications ran through friendly territory. On 27 November, Zhukov met with the *Stavka* to discuss his own operational planning. The latest intelligence reports indicated that strong German resistance would be encountered by Zhukov's spearheads in their westward drive. Zhukov suggested some changes to the operational plan, which Stalin accepted without argument. The revised attack arrangements included in the final plan were later recounted by Zhukov in his memoirs:

> The immediate operational objective of the 1st Byelorussian Front was to break the crust of enemy defence in two different areas simultaneously and, having knocked out the Warsaw-Radom enemy grouping, to move out to the Łódz meridian. The subsequent plan of action was to advance towards Poznan up to the line running through Bromberg-Poznan and further south where tactical contact with the troops of the 1st Ukrainian Front was to be made.

Apart from some minor changes, the *Stavka* plan was formalised following a final review meeting chaired by Stalin in late December. The offensive was scheduled to begin in mid-January. Deception measures (*Maskirovka*) were put into place to confuse German intelligence as to the strength and dispositions of Soviet forces. On Marshal Konev's sector of operations, 400 dummy tanks and 1,000 dummy guns served notice to the Germans that the main thrust from the Sandomierz bridgehead would be in the direction of Krakow. His real intention was to reach the Oder near Breslau, circumvent the industrial region of Silesia, and take the factories and mines intact for future exploitation after the war. Zhukov had far less room to manoeuvre than Konev, and faced the difficult task of breaking through the German defences facing the Magnuszew and Pulawy bridgeheads. Zhukov virtually guaranteed the success of his drive towards Frankfurt-an-der-Oder by achieving a force superiority in the region of 10:1. This force ratio was far in excess of the normal 3:1 ratio generally accepted as the minimum required to achieve success. More than 50 per cent of his rifle divisions and 70 per cent of his armour were crowded into the Magnuszew bridgehead. They waited, tensed like a coiled spring, which would explode with all their pent-up energy when finally released. With such a force, Zhukov was confident of destroying the German defences and of clearing a path through to the Oder.

Meanwhile, in the West, Hitler's desperate thrust towards Antwerp had been blunted. However, the fighting remained heavy as he was not prepared to sanction a withdrawal. On 6 January 1945, Winston Churchill contacted Stalin to enquire about the prospect of accelerating Soviet offensive plans in order to relieve the burden on the Western Front:

> The battle in the West is very heavy and, at any time, large decisions may be called for from the Supreme Command. You know yourself from your own experience how very anxious the position is when a very broad front has to be defended after temporary loss of the initiative. It is General Eisenhower's great desire and need to know in outline what you plan to do, as this obviously affects all his and our major decisions... I shall be grateful if you can tell me whether we can count on a major Russian offensive on the Vistula front, or elsewhere, during January, with any other points you care to mention. I shall not pass this most secret information to anyone except Field Marshal Brooke and General Eisenhower, and only under conditions of the utmost secrecy. I regard the matter as urgent.

On the following day, Stalin assured the British Prime Minister that he would do what he could to ease the situation in the West by saying:

> In view of the position, the supreme command has decided to accelerate the completion of our preparations, and, regardless of the weather, to commence large-scale offensive operations against the Germans along the whole central front not later than the second half of January.

On 8 January, General Antonov contacted the front commanders by radio-telephone with the accelerated offensive schedule. This late change placed extra strain on planners and logistic services. As such, it was inevitable that the Vistula-Oder and East Prussian operations would be launched consecutively rather than simultaneously. It is quite possible that Stalin and the *Stavka* were attempting to synchronise the main assaults. Whatever the reason, Stalin could feel quite satisfied that as far as the Allies were concerned, he was seen to be making the grand gesture by coming to their aid.

Marshal Konev was ordered to commence his assault eight days ahead of schedule on 12 January, regardless of the weather, which had grounded his supporting Air Army. Despite the lack of air support for his offensive, Konev was confident of success as the cold weather hardened the ground, thus greatly easing the movement of vehicles and armour. Zhukov and Rokossovsky were ordered to begin their operations two days later. While the staggering of the main offensive thrusts appeared somewhat untidy, it would have the effect of drawing away German reserves from the crucial central sector to the threatened flanks. Shuffling their limited reserves from one threatened sector to another could only postpone the inevitable collapse of the German defence. The Soviet victory was all but assured.

4

Red Storm on the Oder

On 12 January 1945, Konev opened his offensive with a force that Zhukov considered to be almost as powerful as his own. Indeed, the two fronts were almost equal in strength, with Konev having at his disposal 1,083,800 troops as measured against Zhukov's force of 1,028,900 troops supplemented by the 91,000 troops of the 1st Polish Army. Konev's attack began at 5 a.m. with a thunderous artillery barrage. The storm of steel that descended on the German positions was unleashed by as many as 300 heavy and medium-calibre guns per kilometre of front. The barrage shattered the 4th Panzer Army's communications and broke up mobile reserves stationed close to the main battle line. Following this short but highly effective barrage, forward battalions moved ahead of the main forces and occupied the first and, in some instances, the second line of defences.

Satisfied with his initial progress, Konev then began a second round of artillery preparation. As air support continued to be hampered by the weather, it was more prolonged and elaborate than the first. It started at 10 a.m. with a fifteen-minute deluge of hot steel, followed by forty minutes of more deliberate shelling. This massive strike delivered by guns, which were aligned practically wheel to wheel, was then followed by a short seven-minute barrage, which destroyed the German artillery command network. Another thirty minutes of deliberate fire followed, after which there was a lull. The German defenders thought that the barrage was over and rushed to occupy their firing positions. They were taken by surprise by another intensive barrage and *Katusha* (multiple rocket launcher) strike. The main infantry assault supported by armoured elements then moved forward under the cover of a rolling barrage. The German defences broke, and by the end of the day, Konev's forces had advanced up to 20 kilometres on a 35-kilometre front. By the end of the second day, the penetration had extended to a depth of 40 kilometres. The Germans were on the run. By 18 January, Konev's forces were five days ahead of schedule having seized Czestochowa and encircled Krakow. Two days later, the industrial area around Katowice was abandoned, and as the 3rd Guards Tank Army and elements of the 4th Ukranian Front closed in on the Silesian industrial region in late January, they purposefully left the Germans a 'Golden Bridge' as an escape route. The valuable industries and mines were thus taken intact. Stalin had his 'Gold.'

Zhukov began his main offensive from the Magnuszew bridgehead at 8.30 a.m. on 14 January with a thunderous artillery barrage, which as Chuikov noted, 'Made the earth heave and shake as if in fever.' Instead of the two-and-a-half-hour barrage originally planned, the reconnaissance in force would go in after a twenty-five-minute artillery preparation designed to stun and stupefy the defenders. In total, some 315,000 rounds were dumped on positions occupied by the German 9th Army. The attack went in straight away, and the defenders fell back under the sheer weight of the reconnaissance effort, which far exceeded previous probes, so much so that it was taken to be the main attack. By noon, gaps wide enough for the Soviet armour to advance through had been opened up. By the end of the day, the Pilica river had been crossed and a wedge some 12 kilometres deep had been driven into the German lines.

The attack launched from the Pulawy bridgehead was even more of a success, with troops crossing the Zwolenka river and penetrating German defences to a depth of 22 kilometres on the first day. As German forces were locked into a battle for Radom, Guderian warned Hitler that the Eastern Front could not survive without major reinforcements. There were none

Red Army units crossing the Oder.

forthcoming, for the time being the Eastern Front would have to take care of itself. On 15 January, Soviet fighter-bombers and anti-tank guns broke up a determined German counterattack by the 19th and 25th Panzer Divisions aimed at relieving the shattered remnants facing the Magnuszew bridgehead. After containing the German repost, Zhukov's troops broke out to threaten Łódz and Warsaw. Like a steamroller, the advance moved on, crushing everything in its path. The German defence was effectively shattered, General Kurt von Tippelskirch reporting:

> By the evening of 16 January there was no continued, organically connected German front in the sector between the Rivers Pilica and Nida. The units of the 9th Army still holding on the Vistula near Warsaw and south of it were in grave danger. There were no more reserves.

On 17 January, the 1st Belorussian Front and the 1st Ukrainian Front came abreast of each other. The armour pushed forward, Zhukov later recalling that, 'Our thrust was so swift and so stunning that the Germans abandoned all hope of stopping the Soviet troops anywhere in Poland.' Warsaw was quickly enveloped, resulting in a hasty evacuation, albeit one carried out after an orgy of wanton destruction that reduced the city to ruins. Following the liberation of the ruined capital by troops of the 1st Polish Army, the Military Council of the Front reported to Stalin:

> The fascist barbarians have destroyed Warsaw, capital of Poland. With sadistic cruelty the Hitlerites demolished one block of houses after another. The largest industrial enterprises have been razed to the ground... Thousands upon thousands of civilians have been exterminated, the rest driven out. It is a dead city.

Hitler responded to the loss of Warsaw by lashing out at his own commanders. He also continued to ignore Guderian's increasingly desperate pleas for reinforcements for the central sector. While Hitler became increasingly irrational, Stalin developed a marked tendency towards caution. The fruits of victory were tumbling quickly into his hands, perhaps too quickly, as history had shown that overconfidence could lead to disaster.

A *Stavka* directive issued on 17 January redefined the objectives for the 1st Belorussian Front and 1st Ukrainian Front. Zhukov's objective was to secure the Poznan–Bydgozcz line no later than 2–4 February. Konev's objective was to attack in the direction of Breslau, reaching the Oder no later than 30 January. However, by the end of 18 January, both fronts were in full pursuit of fleeing German forces. The following day, Krakow and Łódz were captured. The German 4th Panzer Army and 9th Army were reduced to a drifting mass of men. Nehring's and von Saucken's beleaguered troops organised themselves into 'Roving Cauldrons' to hold off the red tide and fight their way back to the safety of the German lines. On 20 January, elements of Konev's forces in the form of lead battalions from the 52nd Army and spearheads of the 3rd Guards Tank Army crossed the German frontier at Namslau. On 22 January, the 5th Guards Army seized a bridgehead on the western bank of the Oder following an advance to Oppeln. On the night of 22–23 January, the 16th Guards Mechanised Brigade reached the Oder north of Steinau while the 17th Guards Mechanised Brigade broke through at Goben. By the evening of 23 January, Bromberg had been cleared of German troops, opening the road into Hitler's Reich.

Stalin intervened on 25 January following an intimation by Zhukov that he intended to continue the advance to Kustrin and from there seize a bridgehead on the Oder. Far from convinced, Stalin ordered him to wait, pointing out that his front would be separated from Rokossovsky's forces by more than 150 kilometres if he continued the advance. Rokossovsky's operations in East Prussia would take a further ten days to complete. Zhukov asked permission to continue with the offensive, pointing out that as time passed, 'it will become more difficult for us to penetrate the Miedzyrzecz fortified line.' Stalin agreed to think things over. In the meantime, a reconnaissance group of the 1st Guards Tank Army reached the fortified area and captured a group of German officers and men. Interrogation of the prisoners soon revealed that the line was not yet manned in many places and that units were in the process of moving in to fill the gaps. After appraising Stalin of the situation, Zhukov was given permission to continue his advance, albeit with specific instructions to safeguard his right flank. German resistance on the Miedzyrzecz line was quickly overcome and by 31 January, lead elements of the 2nd Guards Tank Army had reached the Oder near Kustrin. The following day, the 1st Guards Tank Army broke through to the Oder near Frankfurt-an-der-Oder.

5

Tour A: Kienitz–Kustrin–Frankfurt-an-der-Oder–Lebus

Viewpoint (A1): Kienitz: T-34/85 Tank Memorial

Directions: From your Berlin base, take the B1 via Müncheberg to Gusow-Platkow, then take the L334 to Kienitz. The T-34/85 Tank Memorial, commemorating the establishment of the first bridgehead on the western banks of the Oder on 31 January 1945, is located on a square surrounded by roads named Strasse der Befreiung (Liberation Street). For satnav users, enter Strasse der Befreiung, 28, Kienitz, Letschin, Germany.

The capture of Kienitz was carried out by infantry; one would expect therefore that the memorial in the village square would reflect that fact. However, with the twenty-fifth anniversary of the 'liberation' of Kienitz looming, the mayor had other ideas. The T-34/85 Memorial was the brainchild of Emil Kruger (Mayor of Kienitz). He saw a tank as being the ideal monument, stating emphatically, 'a tank, yes, a real tank, that would be something.' As arrangements to procure a tank were put in place, a competition was set up to design a structure on which to mount the tank. Kruger arranged a meeting with Heinz Hoffman (DDR Minister of Defence) in order to ask if a T-34/85 could be made available. Hoffman agreed and passed the matter on to Colonel Siegfried Storbeck who was then on the staff of the 6th *Panzergrenadier* Division based in Neumünster. A T-34/85 was subsequently made available. The existing memorial on the chosen site was demolished in June 1969 to make way for the tank.

The tank was delivered from Görlitz on a low loader on 11 August 1970. After unloading, it drove under its own power to the memorial site. On the following day, the gun barrel was sealed, the hatches welded shut, and all remaining fuel removed. On the thirty-fifth anniversary of the inauguration in 2005, a ceremony took place to honour the much respected former mayor who had been known as *Panzer Emil*. The ravages of time were already

The author standing by the Kienitz T-34 memorial.

Kienitz memorial plaque.

becoming apparent at the time of the ceremony and some work had been undertaken to maintain the tank. However, it was not until September 2014 that a full restoration took place. The work was carried out by restorer Philipp Hann of the Berlin-based metal restoration company Jgnaszewski. He applied new paint to the tank in preparation for commemorative events marking the seventieth anniversary of the end of the war in May 2015. The memorial plaque, which has also been restored reads, '31 January 1945—Kienitz, the first place to be freed from Fascism on our state territory. Glory and honour to the combatants of the 5th Army and 2nd Guards Tank Army.' It should be noted that the term 'our state territory' means Socialist East Germany.

History

Kienitz developed as a fishing village during the thirteenth century. During the Thirty Years War, the village was pillaged by Swedish soldiers. Kienitz recovered and became a significant agricultural area following the reclamation and cultivation of the Oderbruch by Frederick the Great. The area flourished and most inhabitants earned their living by working on the land. In 1837, Johann Gottlieb Koppe built one of the first sugar beet factories in Germany. By 1856, the Kienitz factory was producing 24,500 quintals of sugar, making it a significant manufacturing site. The Koppe family, who owned the business, were renowned philanthropists, whose legacy in Kienitz was celebrated in 2009 during the 775th anniversary of the founding of the village.

Sugar beet production in the area went into decline after the First World War. Thereafter, Kienitz became a backwater, which in some respects served to insulate it from the horrors of war. When the war eventually came to Kienitz, it came suddenly. On the morning of 31 January 1945, elements of General Nikolai Bezarin's 5th Shock Army crossed the frozen Oder to take Kienitz by surprise. Over the course of the day, more units crossed over and expanded the initial lodgement to a width of 6 kilometres and a depth of 2.5 kilometres. Further reinforcements arrived in the form of a motorised battalion of the 219th Tank Brigade. The fragile ice on the Oder rendered the movement and reinforcement of the bridgehead with armour impossible. As such, the lodgement at Kienitz remained vulnerable to German counterattack.

There were no major German formations available to clear the bridgehead. An infantry-tank combat group was hastily assembled and a thrust launched against the Soviet positions on 1 February. The attack was supported by the teenage gunners of the 6th Battery of the 211th Flak Regiment who laid down a barrage. By sheer chance, the attack turned into a meeting engagement as the advancing German troops and armour stumbled into a Soviet attack being launched at the same time. The German assault quickly lost impetus and ground to a halt. Then, the Luftwaffe took on the burden of attempting to reduce the Kienitz bridgehead.

Viewpoint (A2): Kienitz: 1939–1945 Victims Memorial

Directions: Directly opposite T-34/85 Tank Memorial

Air attacks on Kienitz began on 1 February. More attacks followed with the harbour area being given special attention. Those who could, fled. Some inhabitants made it to the nearby villages of Wriezen and Ortwig. Many others tried to escape from the harbour area, but were killed in the heavy aerial bombardments. To commemorate the victims of war, a cross-shaped stone and steel memorial was inaugurated on 17 September 1999 with the following words:

> This monument has been erected for the many thousands of victims of World War Two, which remained unknown, in the villages of the Oderbruch, in the fields, in the woods and meadows and those whose unmarked graves are on the dike and in the stream.

The design by sculptor Roland Rother is simple, but highly effective. Other works by Rother include the memorial at Mallnow and the 'Phoenix' and 'Great Lovers' sculptures in Frankfurt-an-der-Oder.

Viewpoint (A3): Kienitz: Obelisk

Directions: Drive to the far end of the village heading in a southerly direction towards the Oder Dam. There, you will come to a steel obelisk commemorating the establishment of the first Soviet bridgehead across the Oder. For satnav users, enter the nearest address, which is Strasse der Befreiung,1, Kienitz, Letschin, Germany (continue to drive past the hairdressers on the left and follow the road, which then curves to the left around the Oder damm, the obelisk is immediately on the right).

The Obelisk Memorial was inaugurated on 5 November 1987 and commemorates the establishment of the first bridgehead across the Oder on 31 January 1945. The steel monument is engraved with images of the Kienitz region. In addition, the monument is also engraved with a quotation from Karl Wolf, which reads, 'The offensive demands a boundless mass of energy from us in order to bring the Fascist filth to a quicker end.' The monument has suffered from vandalism over the years and as such the inscriptions can be difficult to read. The author of the quotation on the monument was only eight years old when he left Germany to live in Moscow following the coming to power of the National Socialists in 1933. He was the younger brother of future Stasi spymaster Markus Wolf. At the age of seventeen, he joined the

The Oder near Kienitz.

Red Army. Later, he became a film director, chronicling his own experiences in the film *Ich war neunzehn* (*I was Nineteen*). From 1965 until his death in 1982, Wolf was president of the Academy of Arts of the DDR.

Viewpoint (A4): Kustrin (Kostrzyn): King Bastion

Directions: Take the L33, which will take you towards Gorgast. As you pass Fort Gorgast on your right, join the B1 for Kustrin (Kostrzyn) and cross the bridge over the Oder (Odra) into Poland. Heading across the bridge, you will see the fortifications, which have recently been restored. For satnav users, enter Graniczna, 4, Kostrzyn nad Odra, Poland. There is a car park opposite the McDonalds located on Gorzynska, 2, Kostrzyn nad Odra.

In April 2013, Vyacheslav Polovinkin (head of the Russian Defence Ministry office supervising memorials in Poland) confirmed that 431 Soviet soldiers killed during the siege of Kustrin had been disinterred and subsequently reburied in the Cybinka Memorial. Fortress installations, which survived the 1945 siege and post-war demolitions are the Berlin Gate, the Kietz Gate, the August Wilhelm Ravelin, the remains of the Christian Ludwig Ravelin, the Philipp Bastion, and the Brandenburg Bastion. Some remnants of the old town including the foundations of the castle and church were uncovered in the 1990s giving the town the sobriquet of 'The Pompeii of the Oder.'

King Bastion, Kustrin.

History

Kustrin was granted town privileges by the Margrave Albrecht III around the year 1300. The town prospered, largely due to extensive river trade. In 1537, work began on building the fortress, which was composed of four outer and two middle bastions. The work was supervised by Francesco Chiaramella and Roch Guerrini-Linari and was completed in 1590. In 1730, Frederick William I of Prussia imprisoned his eighteen-year-old son in the Kustrin fortress after he had absconded with a childhood friend, Hans Herman von Katte. The future Frederick the Great was captured and arrested for treason. Katte was executed on 6 November 1730. Having forced his son to witness the beheading of his friend, the younger Frederick was pardoned and sent to work in local administration to learn the ways of government.

During the Seven Years War (1753–1760), Kustrin was besieged by Russian forces led by Count William Fermor. In a skilful manoeuvre executed by Frederick II (Frederick the Great), Prussian forces appeared to the rear of Fermor's troops, causing him to withdraw from Kustrin and seek a more advantageous position at Zorndorf. The ensuing Battle of Zorndorf on 25 August 1758 was one of the bloodiest of the era, involving murderous hand-to-hand fighting and high casualties on both sides. Fermor kept possession of the battlefield, but retired the following day, enabling Frederick to claim a victory.

In 1806, the fortress was occupied by the French who remained until the fall of Napoleon in 1814. As the French troops pulled out of Kustrin, the town was deliberately set on fire and suffered extensive damage. After the Franco-Prussian War, outlying fortifications were built at Zorndorf (Sarbinowo), Tschernow (Czarnów), Sapzig (Zabice), and Gorgast.

Kustrin later became an important railway hub with connections to Berlin and Stettin (Szczecin). These railway links took on a new importance in early 1945, the inexorable Soviet advance resulting in a flood of refugees seeking safety from the dreaded Ivan. The first refugee train arrived on 20 January, it was soon followed by others, with desperate civilians travelling in open goods wagons in sub-zero temperatures. Refugees then began arriving by road from East Prussia, West Prussia, Schniedemuhl, and Landsberg. Horses and carts clogged up the streets. The refugees told tales of disaster and devastation. The atrocities carried out by Red Army troops in East Prussia equalled, if not exceeded, the horrors perpetrated by German forces in Russia. For years, Germany had exported terror to the east, now it dawned on the residents of Kustrin that a catastrophe was looming as the Red Army sought revenge.

On 25 January 1945, Hitler declared Kustrin a fortress with the usual orders to hold out to the last man. However, it was a fortress in name only as the available forces were wholly inadequate for the task. The only regular troops immediately available for defence consisted of a mixed bag of depot, training and convalescent troops plus some engineering and artillery units. There was a shortage of heavy weapons and a complete lack of air defence

Fortress Kustrin. (*Marcin Szala, Wikimedia Commons*)

capability, which left the town vulnerable to air attack. Berlin had promised that flak guns would be dispatched, but they did not arrive until 30 January. Two guns were positioned in the Neustadt area, with another in the Altstadt area; all had wide ranging fields of fire and could be used in a ground role.

Defence preparations had hardly begun when elements of the Soviet 219th Tank Brigade burst into the Neustadt on 31 January. This somewhat precipitous attack resulted in the loss of three Lend-Lease Shermans and a Valentine; it was perhaps indicative of the importance attached to the early capture of Kustrin. In his memoirs, Chuikov writes about Kustrin's strategic significance:

> The Oder is a considerable obstacle to troops advancing on Germany from the east, since it covers all the roads to Berlin ... At the confluence of the Oder, and its tributary the Warta, there was the strongest fortified area in Germany, with the fortress town of Kustrin. Kustrin was of great strategic importance, by virtue of both its geographical position and strength of its forts; it lay across the direct routes to Berlin ... Kustrin was rightly called the gateway to Berlin.

Having failed to take Kustrin by storm, elements of the 5th Shock Army and 8th Guards Army laid siege to the citadel. Stalin had been wrongly informed by the 5th Shock Army HQ that Kustrin had fallen in early February. The 'victory' was honoured in Moscow by an artillery salute. It was not until 22 March that the area was finally cut off by Chuikov's forces who then came under attack five days later by a German counter-stroke launched from Frankfurt-an-der-Oder.

The citadel was subjected to a furious air and artillery bombardment on the morning of 29 March. Assault troops stormed the defences, and after a bloody battle the Red Banner was raised on the main ravelin by the men of First Lieutenant of Guards Mikhail Chepanov's platoon (No. 5 Company, 271st Regiment of the 82nd Guards Division). Chepanov was killed in action that day after receiving his third wound (posthumously awarded the title Hero of the Soviet Union). By noon, the fighting was all but over. Chuikov spoke to Zhukov, reporting, 'The Kustrin fortress is taken.' Zhukov enquired, 'Did you give it to them hot?' Chuikov responded, 'As hot as we could ... We have not counted up the dead Nazis, and the prisoners are still coming in. Major Plekin's regiment took 1,760 prisoners.'

Zhukov's reply of, 'Good, thanks' was characteristically short, but revealed his relief that this significant obstacle had at last been removed. Preparations went ahead for the final push, but supply remained a problem as the bridges over the Oder remained a prime target for the Luftwaffe.

After the war, the ruined town was placed under Polish administration and the remaining German population was subsequently expelled. The remnants of the Altstadt, including the castle, were demolished to provide building materials for the reconstruction of Warsaw. During the early period of the

Portrait of Marshal Zhukov by Konstantin Vasilev.

Fortress Kustrin. (*Author's collection*)

Cold War, the town became a military area and access was restricted. Plans to rebuild some of the Altstadt were considered, but as yet remain on hold.

Viewpoint (A5): Frankfurt-an-der-Oder: Soviet Memorial and Cemetery

Directions: Leaving Kustrin (Kostrzyn) take the B1 and then join the B112 for Frankfurt-an-der-Oder. Turn left down Heilbronner Strasse then right down Lindenstrasse (the cemetery comes up on the left). For satnav users, enter Lindenstrasse, 4, Frankfurt (Oder), Germany.

The Soviet Memorial at Frankfurt-an-der-Oder was designed by Nikolai Tomski and was completed in 1947. The memorial replaced a 1925 monument dedicated to the soldiers of Frederick Wilhelm II's *Leibgrenadierregiments* who were killed during the First World War. The original monument featured a soldier in an 'action' pose facing the east, while the Soviet monument presents a soldier in a sentry-like stance facing the west. The inscription on the monument, which is written in Russian, reads, 'To the eternal remembrance of the Soviet Army combatants who gave their lives for the freedom and independence of the USSR.' Later, an inscription in German was added, which reads, 'Your Legacy, Our Obligation.' In 1975, an eternal flame (now extinguished) was added.

View of Frankfurt-Oder.

Following the withdrawal of Russian troops following German reunification, the monument was transferred to the town authorities in a ceremony attended by 500 guests. In 1997, the monument was climbed by members of the Frankfurt/Oder Alpine Club. Three years later it was vandalised by being defaced with a painted swastika. A full restoration took place between 2001 and 2003.

Frankfurt-an-der-Oder is a good place for a spot of late lunch. There are several eateries close to Karl Marx Strasse. For those who wish to sample local cuisine, the *Frankfurter Kartoffelhaus* is a must (Holzmarkt, 7). If you have time to spare, the Memorial and Documentation Centre based in the former Nazi/Stasi prison is worth a visit (Collegienstrasse, 10).

History

On 12 July 1253, Frankfurt-an-der-Oder received its town charter from the Margrave Johann I. The town flourished as it grew to dominate the river trade between Breslau and Stettin. In 1328, a Polish-Lithuanian army besieged the town, but were later defeated. Trade flourished once again and in 1430, Frankfurt-an-der-Oder joined the Hanseatic League. During the Hussite Revolution (1419–1434), the buildings on the Gubener Vorstadt and the Carthusian Monastery were burned to the ground. During the Thirty Years War, a three-day battle was fought for the town. On 14 April 1631, Swedish forces and Scottish auxiliaries led by King Gustavus Adolphus stormed the town. Many of the defenders were mercenaries and refused to fight until they had been paid. Gustavus Adolphus is considered by many to be one of the great military commanders, being especially skilled in the innovative use of combined arms forces. During the Seven Years War, the town was occupied by Russian troops. As peace was restored to the region, trade again flourished and the town became the setting for the second largest trade fair in Germany.

The city of Frankfurt-an-der-Oder largely escaped the ravages of war until April 1945. There were few major industrial installations in the area, and as a consequence air defence was not a priority. RAF Bomber Command attacked the city with a force of twenty-four Lancasters on the night of 15 February 1944. The targets were the Daimler-Benz factory and the rail yards. Fifty-eight people were killed in the raid; damage to the main target areas was slight. As the city was attacked by Allied bombers so infrequently, it became a resettlement area for bombed-out families. By 5 October 1944, there were 5,936 people resettled in the city; that number had increased to 6,625 by 1 December, with two-thirds of them being relocated from Berlin.

Following the Soviet breakthrough from their Polish bridgeheads, Frankfurt-an-der-Oder was given fortress status on 27 January 1945. During February, large numbers of civilians were evacuated from the Dammvorstadt,

Beresinchen and Gubener Vorstadt districts, only those involved in essential war work remaining. On 29 January, Lieutenant General Hermann Meyer-Rabingen was made fortress commandant. Three weeks later, Meyer-Rabingen was replaced by Colonel Ernst Biehler who was later promoted to the rank of *Generalmajor*. On 5 April, Colonel General Gotthard Heinrici attended a military conference held in the *Führerbunker* in Berlin. He put forward the case for the abandonment of the fortress city:

> In the Ninth Army sector, one of the weakest parts of the front is around Frankfurt. The garrison strength is very low, as is their ammunition. I believe we should abandon the defence of Frankfurt and bring the troops out.

Hitler was, of course, unprepared to give up any ground voluntarily and after the arrival of *Reichsmarschall* Herman Goering launched into a diatribe against all those who seemingly did not understand the value of fortresses:

> Again and again, forts have fulfilled their purpose throughout the war. This was proven at Posen, Breslau and Schneidemuhl. How many Russians were pinned down by them? And how difficult they were to capture! Every one of those forts was held to the very last man! History has proved me right and my order to defend a fort to the last man is right! That's why Frankfurt is to retain its status as a fort!

Demanding to know Colonel Biehler's credentials, Hitler snapped, 'Is he a Gneisenau?' Heinrici could only answer, 'The battle for Frankfurt will prove whether he is a Gneisenau or not.' After seeing Biehler in person, Hitler decided he was no Gneisenau and issued orders to have him replaced. Heinrici was enraged by this decision and put up such a powerful defence that a teletype message was received on 7 April reinstating him to his command.

Volkssturm armband. (*Author's collection*)

The forces at Biehler's disposal were weak, consisting of four Fortress Grenadier regiments made up from a mixture of *Volkssturm* and Alarm units, one Fortress Infantry battalion, two Fortress Machine Gun battalions, four Fortress Artillery battalions, one Pioneer battalion, and one Fortress *Panzerjäger* detachment. Biehler's units held their positions, awaiting the inevitable Soviet onslaught.

Following the launch of the Soviet offensive on 16 April, Frankfurt's bridges were blown. Heavy air attacks between 20 and 23 April by the Soviet 3rd Bomber Air Corps destroyed large areas of the city. By this time, the city had been largely abandoned as indefensible and on the morning of 23 April, troops of the 370th Infantry Division of the 69th Army and the 89th Infantry Division of the 33rd Army entered the city.

Viewpoint (A6): Lebus: Soviet Cemetery

Directions: Take the B5 and B112 to Lebus. At the roundabout, take the first exit onto Strasse der Freiheit, then turn left onto Lindenstrasse, turn right onto Postberg where you will see the cemetery on the right. For satnav users, enter Postberg, 1, Lebus, Germany.

Lebus Soviet Cemetery and Memorial.

The Soviet Cemetery at Lebus contains the remains of 4,534 soldiers who fell in battle. In September 2012, a service of reconciliation was held at the cemetery following the reinterment of fifty-six Soviet soldiers. On 8 May 2015, German President Joachim Gauck attended a commemoration event marking the seventieth anniversary of the end of the Second World War. Gauck hailed the 'liberation' of Germany from Nazi tyranny in a widely reported speech in which he paid tribute to 'victims of violence and war':

> The Second World War ended seventy years ago today. It was a war started by Germany, and it brought immeasurable suffering to millions of people all over the world. The war did not end because Germany itself found the strength to throw off the shackles of the Nazi dictatorship. It ended because Germany was defeated militarily by the Allied forces. By its end, the war had claimed millions of victims, not only soldiers of many nationalities, but also civilians, including women and children. Disproportionately many died in the final days of the war ... I bow low in remembrance of their suffering, and the suffering and service of those who fought Hitler's Germany and liberated Germany... We pay tribute to all those victims of violence and war who lost their lives at that time. We grieve with all those who have from that day forth grieved for the dead and the missing.

The author at Lebus Soviet Cemetery.

Gauck's speech can be traced back to one made by President Richard von Weizsacker on 8 May 1985 in which he defined the anniversary as a 'day of liberation.' He succeeded in exploding the myths that served the older generation as their means of avoiding responsibility for crimes committed in their name:

> Many nations are today commemorating the date on which World War II ended in Europe. Every nation is doing so with different feelings, depending on its fate ... We Germans are commemorating that date amongst ourselves, as is indeed necessary. We must find our own standards. We are not assisted in this task if we or others spare our feelings ... For us, the 8th May is above all a date to remember what people had to suffer ... The greater honesty we show in commemorating this day, the freer we are to face the consequences with due responsibility. For us Germans, 8 May is not a day of celebration ... Most Germans had believed that they were fighting and suffering for the good of their country. And now it turned out that their efforts were not only vain and futile, but had served the inhuman goals of a criminal regime ... Looking back, they saw the dark abyss of the past, and looking forward, they saw an uncertain, dark future. Yet with every day something became clearer, and this must be stated on behalf of us all today: the 8th May was a day of liberation. It liberated all of us from the inhumanity and tyranny of the National-Socialist regime ... We commemorate the six million Jews who were murdered in German concentration camps. We commemorate all nations who suffered in the war, especially the countless citizens of the Soviet Union and Poland who lost their lives... There is no such thing as the guilt or innocence of an entire nation. Guilt is, like innocence, not collective, but personal ... Everyone who directly experienced that era should today quietly ask himself about his involvement then... The vast majority of today's population were either children then or had not been born. They cannot profess a guilt of crimes they did not commit. No discerning person can expect them to wear a penitential robe simply because they are Germans. But their forefathers have left them a grave legacy. All of us, whether guilty or not, whether old or young, must accept the past ... If we for our part sought to forget what has occurred, instead of remembering it, this would not only be inhuman, we would also impinge upon the faith of the Jews who survived and destroy the basis of reconciliation. We must erect a memorial to thoughts and feelings in our own hearts ... On this 8th May, let us face up as well as we can to the truth.

Weizsacker's speech was hailed by *The New York Times* as a 'sober message of hope to the uneasy generation of young West Germans.' However, the Christian Social Union party objected the phrase 'day of liberation', instead referring to 8 May as 'a day of deepest humiliation.' In 1986, German Green Party politician and activist Petra Kelly said that the speech made by

Weizsacker was, 'correct, but not more than self-evident.' The speech was issued as a vinyl record, selling more than 60,000 copies.

History

The area formerly known as Lubusz Land was brought under Polish control in the year 966, during the reign of Mieszko I. A castle was built as a shield against German invasion; the strategic importance of Lebus was later noted in the thirteenth-century chronicles which refer to the area as the 'key to the kingdom of Poland.' The Bishopric of Lebus was founded during the reign of Boleslaw III Krzyousty (1086–1138) to convert the West Slavic Polabian Tribes. In 1163, the Holy Roman Emperor Frederick I granted property rights in the Lubusz Land to the Silesian Piasts. German colonisation of the area followed and Lebus as it was now known was granted town privileges by Duke Henry I of Silesia in 1226. During the Middle Ages, Lebus developed as an important stop on the trade routes between the Baltic and Italy. However, trade stagnated following political and religious changes in the sixteenth century, which reduced Lebus to the state of an economic backwater. In 1701, Lebus was incorporated into the Kingdom of Prussia. After the Napoleonic Wars, it came under the administration of the Province of Brandenburg.

Viewpoint (A7): Lebus: Ruined Church and German War Graves

> Directions: Head out of Lebus east on the B167, then head in a southerly direction on the L383 (follow signs for Boossen/Walków/Schönfließ). Carry on past Weisenweg; the church then comes up on your left. For satnav users, enter Schönfließer Dorfstrasse, 17, Lebus, Germany.

In February 1945, German troops blew up the church tower, which was being used as an aiming point by Soviet artillery. The church suffered further damage by shelling in April 1945, which left only the outer walls standing. Since 1945, the site has been preserved as a semi-ruin. Fourteen German war graves are located in the well-kept church grounds.

6

Controversies and Opportunities

In late January, the *Stavka* still looked towards an early assault on Berlin as evidenced by the rapid approval of both Zhukov's plan of attack on 27 January and Konev's plan two days later. By 3 February, Zhukov's forces had succeeded in strengthening their lodgements on the western banks of the Oder. However, German troops still hung on to their own bridgeheads at Frankfurt-an-der-Oder and Kustrin, threatening Zhukov's line of advance. Zhukov began to look towards his extended front and flanks with a degree of anxiety, noting that Rokossovsky's forces were still lagging behind and that Konev's forces were stymied by the massive obstacle, which Breslau represented.

There were unmistakable signs that German resistance was stiffening in late January. German garrisons held out stubbornly in Thorn, Schneidemuhl, and Poznan. Soviet radio intercepts also began picking up increased signals traffic from the 11th SS Army and 3rd Panzer Army that appeared to indicate an imminent German counter thrust from East Pomerania and Silesia. On 31 January, Zhukov sent an urgent signal to Stalin stressing the vulnerability of his northern flank. The *Stavka* response to Zhukov's concerns was somewhat ambiguous, reflecting a situation in which the higher leadership did not appear fully cognisant of the speed and full extent of their own advances. It was therefore inevitable that a degree of confusion regarding priorities would emerge, as evidenced by Zhukov's specific instructions for the 5th Shock Army to dig in, while at the same time, planning for offensive operations still went ahead.

As late as 8 February, the *Stavka* remained optimistic that operations by Konev's forces in Lower Silesia could be carried out simultaneously with Zhukov's planned drive on Berlin. However, increasing concerns regarding the 'balance of forces', coupled with increased German aerial activity, led to a reordering of priorities, with Rokossovsky's forces being directed to clear German forces from Pomerania and advance as far as Stettin. The anticipated attack against Zhukov's right flank was launched on 16 February, further

German refugees. (*Author's collection*)

Portrait of Marshal Zhukov by Vasili Nikolaevich Yakolev.

convincing the *Stavka* of the need to fully clear the flanks before carrying out a drive on Berlin. Therefore, it is likely that the final decision to bring the Vistula-Oder operation to an end was taken as late as 16 February.

Much ink has been spilled by historians over the years debating whether the Red Army could have taken Berlin off the march in February. Of course, we can never really know what the outcome would have been, but we can consider the arguments put forward by the main protagonists in the February controversy. Chuikov certainly believed that Berlin could have been taken in February and argued his case vociferously:

> In eighteen days we had covered over 50 kilometres, without halt and fighting all the way, thus achieving a strategic leap forward of great length and speed. And if Supreme Command and the Headquarters of the various fronts had organised supply properly and had been able to get the necessary amounts of ammunition, fuel and stores up to the Oder, if the air force had moved up to airfields near the Oder in time, and bridge-building and pontoon units had been there to ensure the passage of troops across the Oder, then our four Armies, the 1st and 2nd Tank Armies could have developed the offensive further, to Berlin, at the beginning of February; they could have covered the remaining 80–100 kilometres and crowned this gigantic operation by the capture of the German capital.

Zhukov strongly disagreed with Chuikov, pointing to his own supply difficulties, urgent maintenance requirements, dispersal of units to counter threats on his flanks and the arrival of German reinforcements along the Oder in the form of the 5th SS Mountain Corps. In his memoirs, Zhukov refuted Chuikov's claims, stating:

> How could the Soviet Command take the risk of continuing the Berlin offensive with such a grave danger looming in the north? War experience shows that taking risks is advisable, but one should not overreach oneself. In this respect, the lesson learned by the Red Army during the Warsaw offensive in 1920 is very instructive, when its headlong, unprotected advance led, instead of success, to the overwhelming defeat of our Western Front ... Chuikov believes that the 1st Byelorussian and the 1st Ukrainian Fronts could detach from three to four armies, including three or four tank armies, to advance on Berlin in February 1945 ... As of February 1, infantry divisions were on the average, 5,500 strong, but, for instance the 8th Guards had only from 3,800 to 4,800 officers and men. The number of tanks in the two tank armies was 740, an average of forty per brigade, whereas in fact many brigades had only between fifteen and twenty tanks... To top everything off, the fortress and the city of Poznan, deep in the rear of the front, was still held by the enemy.

Zhukov goes on to repudiate Chuikov's assertion that poor organisation was responsible for the decision to bring the Vistula-Oder operation to a premature end. Turning Chuikov's argument on its head, Zhukov asserts that speculation regarding supposed organisational shortcomings should not be taken seriously:

> Chuikov's admission that supplies were disorganised and that the air force and pontoon bridge-building units had lagged behind, points to the fact that in the circumstances it would have been utterly adventurist to launch a decisive offensive on Berlin. It follows that neither the 1st Ukrainian Front nor the 1st Byelorussian Front could conduct the Berlin operation in February 1945.

In a sense, further speculation concerning the February controversy is pointless, as in the end it was Stalin who made the final decision. It was one which suited his political agenda of occupying as much territory as possible before imposing Communist rule. A total collapse of Hitler's Germany in February 1945 would not tie in with Stalin's vision of a Communist dominated Eastern Europe dancing to Moscow's tune.

On the night of 31 January, rain began to fall along the central sector of the Oder line. Over the following days, an early thaw set in, melting the snow and ice. In Berlin, Goebbels' chief press aide, Wilfred von Oven, noted how the sudden change in the weather signalled a change for the better in the threatening situation in the east. His diary entry for 1 February reads:

> The formerly threatening situation before Berlin has changed in our favour literally overnight. The splashing in the gutters sounds to our ears like the choirs of angels. The Oder and the Warthe, and the marshes of those two rivers and the Netze, together with a multitude of little water-courses, have become obstacles which enable us to concentrate our defence on the threatened sectors.

The Oder ice melted at a satisfying rate, prompting Himmler to talk of a 'miracle.' The Germans themselves contributed to further speeding up the process by using explosives. The thaw turned dirt roads in Poland into quagmires, further disrupting the flow of supplies to the Soviet Fronts, whose logistical umbilical cord was already stretched to its limit. The thaw gave Hitler a moat and above all bought time in which the defences on the crucial central sector could be bolstered. On 3 February, another diary entry by von Oven noted with some satisfaction the progress being made with defensive preparations during the unseasonably mild weather: 'The thaw continues. Mild spring air wafts through the streets of Berlin, and everywhere we are working energetically to build anti-tank obstacles and emplacements for the anti-tank guns.'

More than 300 flak units armed with the highly effective 88-mm gun were rushed to the front to form an anti-tank screen on the eastern approaches to Berlin. Substantial reinforcements of troops and armour were also rushed to the threatened sector; within two weeks of the onset of the thaw, some fourteen German divisions barred the way to Berlin.

The decision by the *Stavka* to concentrate on securing the flanks before undertaking the main Berlin operation resulted in a weakening of Zhukov's spearhead forces. The window of opportunity for exploiting the more favourable situation, brought about by apparent Soviet indecision was extremely narrow. General Heinz Guderian argued the case for a timely counterstroke against the vulnerable Soviet bridgeheads on the central sector. His original concept was a bold manoeuvre involving enveloping attacks by 6th SS Panzer Army from the northeast and armoured units from the southeast. However, Hitler was reluctant to consider the proposal as he was focused on relieving Budapest and retaining the Hungarian oil-fields and refineries. To this end, he dispatched the 6th SS Panzer Army to Hungary, effectively rendering this powerful force *hors de combat* until such time as its extensive movement by rail was completed.

Having been baulked by Hitler's intransigence concerning the transfer of vital forces to Hungary, Guderian nonetheless continued to attempt to wear Hitler down by repeatedly stating his case that the Oder was the only sector that really mattered. During the evening military conference on 8 February, he strenuously argued for the evacuation of German forces in Courland in order to accumulate sufficient counterattack forces. Their heated exchange proceeded as follows:

> Guderian: You must believe me when I say it is not just pig-headedness on my part that makes me keep on proposing the evacuation of Courland. I can see no other way left to us of accumulating reserves, and without reserves we cannot hope to defend the capital. I assure you that I am acting solely in Germany's interests.
>
> Hitler: How dare you speak to me like that! Don't you think that I am fighting for Germany! My whole life has been one long struggle for Germany.

The argument became so heated that Goering had to step in and physically separate the two protagonists, by taking Guderian by the arm and leading him off to an anteroom. The bizarre scenes at the conference were indicative of the gradual disintegration of the state, its leaders pondering the very real and terrifying prospect of Soviet domination of German lands.

As his relationship with Hitler deteriorated, and with it any prospect of obtaining substantial reserves, Guderian reluctantly abandoned his plans for an envelopment, instead focusing on a single thrust from Stargard. A more limited counterstroke was more to Hitler's taste and he subsequently gave cautious agreement to the Stargard proposal. On 13 February, Guderian attended a further conference, determined to get his own way regarding both the timing of the attack and its professional coordination. The conference was held in the afternoon in the remains of the badly scarred New Chancellery. This was no doubt a welcome change from the claustrophobic atmosphere of the bunker.

The conference began with reports on the general situation by General Alfred Jodl. Guderian then took centre stage. Without preamble, he launched into his arguments for attacking Zhukov's lead forces before their position was fully consolidated. It immediately became apparent that Himmler's army group had no intention of attacking, the excuse put forth by him being that his units were still waiting for all the necessary fuel and ammunition. Guderian pressed the issue and as such the scene was set for another stormy conference scene:

> Guderian: We can't wait until the last can of petrol and the last shell have been issued! By that time the Russians will be too strong.
>
> Hitler: I will not allow you to accuse me of procrastination.
>
> Guderian: I'm not accusing you of anything. I'm simply saying there's no sense in waiting until the last lot of supplies has been issued and the favourable moment to attack has been lost.
>
> Hitler: I've just told you that I won't allow you to accuse me of procrastinating.

The argument concerning the timing of the attack was clearly going nowhere. Nonetheless, Guderian remained unbowed and swiftly moved on to the second strand of his argument:

> Guderian: I want General Wenck at Army Group Vistula as chief of staff. Otherwise there can be no guarantee that the attack will be successful. The man can't do it. How could he do it?'
>
> Hitler: The Reichsführer is man enough to lead the attack on his own.
>
> Guderian: The Reichsführer doesn't have the experience or the right staff to lead the attack without help. The presence of General Wenck is absolutely necessary.
>
> Hitler: How dare you criticise the Reichsführer, I won't have you criticise him!
>
> Guderian: I must insist that General Wenck be transferred to the staff of Army Group Vistula to lead the attack properly.

At this point, Hitler lost his temper completely, Guderian recalling that, 'He was almost screaming, his eyes seemed about to pop out of his head and the veins stood out on his temples.' For the next two hours Guderian repeated his arguments. Then, without warning, Hitler suddenly caved in and acceded to

Marshal Zhukov.

Guderian's demands. Taking him by the arm, he said in a much calmer voice, 'The General Staff has won a battle this day.' *Generalfeldmarschall* Wilhelm Keitel and the other senior officers present berated Guderian for openly contradicting and irritating Hitler. Guderian eyed them with barely concealed contempt and, turning to Wenck, issued orders for the attack to begin in two days.

In what must be considered a remarkable feat of organisation, two corps headquarters and eleven divisions were assembled for the attack. However, concentrating and supplying such a force was virtually impossible due to shortages and limited rail capacity. Indeed, by the eighth day of the assembly, less than half the trains had arrived. Further delays, including the late arrival of the 163rd Infantry Division, meant that not all of the units were in their jump-off positions. After having inspected the attack preparations in person on 13 February, Wenck decided he had no other option than to launch his attack in a piecemeal fashion, beginning with a one division thrust towards Arnswalde. This unpromising compromise, which largely came about to satisfy Guderian's desire to avoid delay, did not augur well for success.

Soviet intelligence made Zhukov aware of the probability of a German attack. However, he still lacked detailed information regarding its timing and objectives. Consequently, the one division attack carried out by the 11th SS *Panzergrenadier* Division Nordland achieved complete tactical surprise, resulting in a break through to Arnswalde and the relief of its beleaguered garrison. Hot on the heels of this early success, elements of the 11th SS Panzer Army attacked the following day and recaptured Pyritz. The hastily assembled and relatively inexperienced units committed to the attack failed to consolidate their early gains. Consequently, they lost momentum, due to a combination of stubborn resistance and the thaw that turned the battlefield into a quagmire.

On 17 February, Wenck was seriously injured in a car accident while returning to the front after a briefing meeting with Hitler in Berlin. His replacement, General Hans Krebs ordered the attack to continue, but the initiative had been lost. Zhukov redeployed the 3rd Shock Army, which effectively blunted the German drive. At best, the 11th SS Panzer Army penetrated to a depth of 8 kilometres. Losses in men and materiel were heavy. On 18 February, a 'directive for regroupment' was issued, bringing the shortest and least successful of German offensive operations to an ignominious end.

Following the costly failure of Operation Solstice, all the signs pointed to an impending Soviet drive on Berlin by Zhukov's and Konev's fronts. Unbeknown to the Germans, their hastily conceived and badly executed offensive had an impact on Soviet operational thinking, which was totally out of proportion to the actual results achieved on the ground. The surprise German attack prompted the *Stavka* into considering the need to clear the flanks before launching the drive on Berlin. Between 17 and 22 February, Zhukov and Rokossovsky received orders to launch a joint attack aimed at Kolberg, Danzig, and Gdynia. Rokossovsky would attack first on 24 February, followed by Zhukov who would launch his own assault no later than 1 March. Rokossovsky attacked on schedule and, within two days, had smashed through the German defences on a 50-kilometre front, penetrating to a depth of 45 kilometres.

Zhukov attacked on 1 March, his leading armoured elements heading northwards, perplexing the German military leaders who had fully expected a full blooded drive on Berlin. By 5 March, Stargard and Kolberg had been reached. Refugees took to the roads in a desperate attempt to escape the rapidly advancing Red Army. Safety was an illusion, as Rokossovsky's forces had reached the Gulf of Danzig by 25 March; on the following day, Gdynia fell. By 30 March, Danzig had been cleared of German troops.

Meanwhile, to the south, Konev launched an attack on 8 February from his bridgeheads astride Breslau, which aimed at occupying western Silesia and bringing his forces abreast of the 1st Belorussian Front on the River Neisse. Within three days, his forces had opened a massive breach of over 140 kilometres. Penetrating to a depth of sixty kilometres, Konev's forces then cut off the German garrison at Glogau before pushing on to the Neisse. By 13 February, Breslau was surrounded and besieged by the 6th Army. The Luftwaffe began air drops two days later and, over the next seventy-six days, flew more than 2,000 sorties in support of the doomed fortress.

Colonel General Gotthard Heinrici. (*Hermann Historica International Auctioneers*)

For Germany, the decision of the Red Army to halt on the Oder appeared to signal a lifeline. Would the West finally come to its senses and realise that the Soviet Union was the real enemy? Wiser heads dismissed such wishful thinking and saw the lull along the Oder for what it was—a temporary reprieve. Guderian still believed that much could be gained from buying time. However, he was acutely aware that time was running short and therefore the replacement of the dilettante commander of Army Group Vistula was a matter of the utmost priority. On 19 March, Guderian set out for Himmler's headquarters in order to convince him to relinquish his command. It transpired that Himmler was not at his headquarters, but at a clinic in Hohenlychen recovering from a nervous collapse. Guderian expressed sympathy and suggested that the burden of holding down so many offices would 'surely tax the strength of any man.' Guderian had little trouble in persuading Himmler to give up his command, as he was clearly looking for a way out. In a diary entry dated 21 March, Goebbels wrote:

> I hear Himmler wishes to give up his Army Group Vistula and he should do so. Himmler's job, after all, was merely to plug a hole in the area of Army Group Vistula the best he could. Unfortunately he allowed himself to be diverted by the quest for military laurels, in which, however, he failed totally.

Goebbels' assessment was quite correct in that Himmler was transfixed by the idea of being awarded the Knight's Cross. He was therefore more than glad to be relieved of the burden of commanding an army group, which in reality was very different from his fantasy visions of martial glory.

Hitler readily acquiesced to Guderian's proposal to replace Himmler with General Gotthard Heinrici, a noted expert in defence, who had achieved notable successes while commanding 1st Panzer Army in Hungary. Heinrici later recalled the circumstances of his appointment and his reaction to it in a post-war interview:

> On 20 March 1945 I received a telephone report that I had been appointed to the command of *Heeresgruppe Weichel.* Up to that time I had been in command of the 1. *Panzerarmee* which in February and March, had been engaged in heavy fighting with the Russians who were attempting to to burst into the area around Cosel driving in the general direction of Leobschutz and on to Troppau and thence to occupy the rest of Upper Silesia which remained in German hands. At the report of my appointment I was extremely surprised. It was certainly known to me that I was hardly *persona grata* with Hitler.

It could be argued that Hitler's acceptance of Heinrici was a reflection of his understanding of the grim military realities that faced him, following the successive failures of the Ardennes offensive in the West and the Danube offensive in Hungary. Realising that the cupboard was now bare, he was nonetheless determined to hold on in the hope that something would turn up.

On the morning of 22 March, Heinrici made his way down Reichstrasse 96 to Zossen in order to formally take up his appointment as commander of Army Group Vistula. He knew little about the formation he was taking over, but was sure that Guderian would fully put him in the picture. Heinrici met with Guderian in his office, which was located within the Maybach I complex. After the usual pleasantries, Heinrici got straight down to business by saying, 'General, I've been in the wilds of Hungary. I know almost nothing about Army Group Vistula, what it's composed of, or what the situation is on the Oder.' Guderian replied candidly, holding nothing back. The picture he painted of the situation was grim:

> The Russians are looking down our throats. They've halted their offensive to reorganise and regroup. We estimate that you'll have three to four weeks, until the floods go down, to prepare. In that time the Russians will try to establish new bridgeheads on the western bank and broaden those they already have. These have to be thrown back. No matter what happens elsewhere, the Russians must be stopped on the Oder. It's our only hope.

Then, after having called for maps, Guderian outlined what Heinrici later described as, 'the whole shocking truth'. Germany was being gradually swallowed up with each successive push by the Allies in the west and the Red Army in the east. The war in the west was clearly lost, the Americans having seized and consolidated a bridgehead on the eastern bank of the Rhine. All that was left was to hold off the Soviets as long as possible in the hope that the western Allies would take Berlin first.

To hold back the might of the massive Red Army force building up on the Oder, Heinrici had at his disposal the 3rd Panzer Army, commanded by General Hasso von Manteuffel, and the 9th Army, commanded by General Theodor Busse. Between them, the two formations covered a front of 281 kilometres stretching from the Baltic coast to the confluence of the Oder and the Neisse in Silesia. Heinrici's strongest force was Busse's 9th Army, which had succeeded in maintaining communications with Kustrin along a single narrow corridor. Just as Heinrici was coming to grips with the tactical situation, Guderian delivered a piece of shattering news: 'Hitler has decided to launch an attack to wipe out the bridgehead south of Kustrin and General Busse has been preparing. I believe it's to take place within forty-eight hours.'

Heinrici studied the situation map and quickly concluded that the attack would fail. Noting that the sector between Frankfurt-an-der-Oder and Kustrin was heavily defended, he warned Guderian that, 'Our troops will be pinned with their backs to the Oder. It will be a disaster.' Guderian said nothing, but invited Heinrici to the military conference in Berlin where the Kustrin attack was to be discussed. Heinrici declined by saying, 'If I'm supposed to launch this insane attack the day after tomorrow, I'd better get to my headquarters as soon as possible. Hitler can wait a few days to see me.'

Heinrici was driven to Himmler's 'Birkenwald' headquarters at Birkenheim. There he met with the outgoing commander of Army Group Vistula who subjected him to an excruciating speech of self-justification, one mercifully cut short by an urgent telephone call from General Busse. Himmler picked up the phone, listened in silence for a few minutes, and then handed the receiver to Heinrici, saying, 'You're the new commander, you'd better take this.' Busse reported, 'The Russians have broken through and have enlarged their bridgehead near Kustrin.' Heinrici relayed the information to Himmler who coolly replied, 'Well, you're the new commander of Army Group Vistula. Issue the proper orders.' This was all too much for Heinrici who retorted, 'I don't know a damn thing about the army group. I don't even know what troops I have or who's supposed to be where.' Himmler said nothing. Clearly, Himmler had abdicated all responsibility, and as such, no help could be expected from him. In the circumstances, all Heinrici could do was to tell Busse to issue orders as he felt best in the current situation.

Advance on Frankfurt and Berlin

(Story on page 1.)

Red Army advances: *Chicago Daily Tribune*, 2 April 1945. (*Author's collection*)

That evening, Himmler and his staff departed for the West. Indeed, their departure was so complete that it seemed to Heinrici that it had all been a horrible dream and that Himmler had never been there at all. With the 'Birkenwald' now vacated, Heinrici could concentrate on the difficult problem of defending a long front line with inadequate forces. His difficulties were compounded by Hitler's insistence that the next Soviet drive would be aimed at Prague and not Berlin. Having had his operational reserves removed, Heinrici was left with a miscellany of units with names that were totally unfamiliar. Besides being short of combat trained troops, crippling supply shortages meant that some replacements were arriving at the front armed only with the single shot *Panzerfaust* anti-tank weapon. Heinrici's operations officer, Colonel Hans Georg Eismann flared up on hearing the news, declaring that, 'It's madness. How are these men supposed to fight after they fire their one round? What does OKH expect them to do—use their empty weapons like billy clubs? It's mass murder.' Heinrici could only agree and set about rectifying the situation as best he could.

Heinrici's immediate concern was the situation at Kustrin. On 23 March, General Busse launched two attacks aimed at relieving the garrison, which was in danger of being totally cut off. Both attacks failed due to determined Soviet resistance and ended in heavy losses. Busse attacked again on 27 March. This time, some tanks actually managed to break through into the town. However, the attack stalled and the attacking forces were smashed by artillery fire. The failure of the Kustrin relief effort resulted in wild scenes at the military conference on 28 March, culminating in Guderian's dismissal by Hitler. With Guderian gone, so too was any prospect of the German higher command excercising sound military judgement.

Heinrici knew that he would receive little support from Guderian's successor, General Hans Krebs who was a career officer and a staunch Hitler loyalist. Eismann summed up the general feeling about Krebs within the army group:

> This man, with his eternally friendly smile, reminded me somewhat of a fawn... It was clear what we could expect. Krebs had only to spout a few confident phrases—and the situation was rosy again. Hitler would get much better support from him than from Guderian.

Without the support of Guderian's forthright opinions at the military conference on 5 April, Heinrici nonetheless managed to argue his case by vigorously challenging Hitler's ridiculous assertion that the Soviet forces were almost exhausted. The heavy dose of realism injected into the conference proceedings by Heinrici was a revelation:

My *Führer*, the Russian forces are both capable and enormous ... I must tell you, that since the transfer of the armoured units to Schorner, all my troops—good and bad—must be used as front line troops. There are no reserves. None. Will they resist the heavy shelling preceding the attack? Will they withstand the initial impact? For a time, perhaps, yes. But, against the kind of attack we expect, every one of our divisions will lose a battalion a day. This means that along the whole battlefront we will lose divisions themselves at the rate of one per week. We cannot sustain such losses. We have nothing to replace them with. My *Führer*, the fact is that, at best, we can hold out for just a few days. Then, it must all come to an end.

German propaganda from 1945: 'Total war, shortest war!' (*Author's collection*)

Heinrici's performance at the conference served to underscore the understated yet professional demeanour that Hitler came to respect. Heinrici won the argument to establish a multi-layered defence based around the Seelow Heights. Hitler's endorsement of Heinrici's defence plan, which ran contrary to current practice, speaks volumes about the level of trust placed in this highly energetic and competent commander who within a few short weeks of his appointment had transformed the German defence on the crucial Oder Front. The Red Army were in for a hard fight on the easterly approaches to Berlin.

7

Tour B: Wünsdorf–Zossen

Viewpoint (B1): Wünsdorf: Zeppelin Bunker Complex

> Directions: From your Berlin base, take the B96a to Baumschulenstrasse, then join the A113 from Spathstrasse. Continue on A113 along Neue Spathstrasse, then turn left down Baumschulenweg. Continue down the A113 in the direction of Mittenwalde, then join the Schenkendorfer Chaussee. Continue along the Schenkendorfer Chaussee and then take the B246 and B96 to the Bunker site. For satnav users, enter Guthenbergstrasse Strasse 1, Wünsdorf (Zossen), Germany. Parking is available further up the road on Zeppelinstrasse.

The bunker complex at Wünsdorf is administered by Bücherstadt-Tourismus who run five different tours covering the site. Tour 1 is the most accessible and runs all year round. This one-and-a-half-hour guided tour costs 12 Euro per head and covers the Maybach 1 and Zeppelin complexes; it runs weekdays Tuesday–Friday at 2 p.m., on weekends and holidays in May–September at 12 p.m., 2 p.m., and 4 p.m., and on weekends and holidays in October–April at 1 p.m. and 3 p.m. Other tours available include the 'Four Bunker Tour' and the 'On the marks of the Russians' tour. Apart from Tour 1, all other tours need to be booked in advance: phone +49 (0) 33 702 96 00.

Wünsdorf is an official member of the International Organisation of Book Towns based on the Hay-on-Wye model. There are three large bookshops on site; the 'Bunker Shop' will be of particular interest as it specialises in military literature. It also has for sale an interesting range of militaria, including headgear, uniforms, and decorations. There are three eateries on site: for those with a liking for Greek food, there is the 'Restaurant Akropolis'; those wishing to sample more regional fare should head to the 'Waldstadt Treff', which is located in the former imperial stables; and the Teestubchen offers a wide variety of speciality teas and Russian biscuits.

Pneumatic messaging system at Zossen.

Zossen bunker ruins.

History

In 1871, the Prussian Army established a shooting range at Kummersdorf. Sixteen years later, a rail link was built to connect it with another range at Jüterbog. The following year, Zossen's train station opened on the main Berlin to Dresden line. Along with paying passengers, military traffic also passed through Zossen *en route* to the military training areas. In 1910, a proving ground and garrison were established in the Waldstadt area of Wünsdorf. Over the next four years, the site developed into Europe's largest military base, covering an area of 60,000 acres. During the First World War, several prisoner of war camps were constructed in the area, including the 'Crescent' camp, which was the brainchild of diplomat and propagandist Max von Oppenheim. The camp housed between 4,000–5,000 Muslim prisoners who had fought for the Allies, along with eighty Sikh prisoners and approximately fifty Irishmen. Oppenheim hoped to stir up anti-British sentiment among the prisoners in the so-called 'Jihad Experiment.' Approximately 3,000 prisoners were recruited to fight against the British in Africa and the Middle East. Low morale led to numerous desertions, and the experiment was wound up in 1917. Roger Casement had more success in recruiting men from the Irish contingent for the Irish Brigade. However, the German authorities lost enthusiasm for the venture following the failure of the Easter Rising in Dublin and Casement's subsequent capture.

Wünsdorf remained an important military area following the establishment of the Weimar Republic Army, and by 1931, was home to a motorised division. Following the rise of the National Socialist Party to power in 1933, the military area was further developed and became the setting for the establishment of the first panzer divisions. In 1935, the High Command relocated to Wünsdorf. Priority was then given to the construction of the Zeppelin communications complex. The completed telex bunker, also known as 'Amt 500', covered an area of 4,881 square metres on two levels and was protected against air attack by thick blast proof concrete walls and ceilings. Work on the Maybach 'I' and II complexes commenced in 1938 and was centred on a unique concept in which the rooms above ground were duplicated in the underground levels, meaning that in the event of an air raid, work could continue undisturbed. The construction work on Maybach 'I' was completed in time for the High Command to move in during the run up to the invasion of Poland. Work on Maybach II was not completed until the early summer of 1940.

Allied intelligence only really became aware of the significance of the military compound at Wünsdorf in early 1944, following the capture of a German Sergeant in Italy who had previously served at Maybach 'I.' The camp complex was subsequently bombed, the heaviest attack being delivered by 675 American bombers on 15 March 1945. Approximately 120 people were killed in the raid, and General Krebs received a head wound. Communications from the complex were only disrupted for two hours. The largely intact military area continued to function right up until the sighting of advance units of General Pavel Rybalko's 3rd Guards Tank Army on 20 April necessitated an evacuation of the main staff. As the column of retreating vehicles made its way to the relative safety of Wannsee, they were mistakenly attacked by German aircraft.

The Zeppelin complex was taken intact. Major Boris Polevoy, a political commissar and *Pravda* reporter attached to Konev's headquarters staff, was taken on a tour of the complex by chief engineer Hans Beltow. Large signs attached to the telephone switchboards warned in schoolboy Russian, 'Soldiers! Do not damage this equipment, it will be valuable to the Red Army.' Much of the valuable equipment was later dismantled and sent to the Soviet Union, where Stalin wanted a similar complex built for himself. The two Maybach bunkers were made unfit for military use. However, the Zeppelin bunker was retained and later re-equipped as a communications centre. In 1971, the Soviet 16th Air Army based itself at the Zeppelin complex and the site and surrounding areas subsequently became known as 'Little Moscow.' When the Soviets finally pulled out of the area in 1994, they left behind 45,000 cubic metres of hazardous waste including asbestos. Today, the only reminder of the Soviet presence is the rather forlorn looking statue of Lenin, which stands outside of the former Army Sports School/Officers' House.

Viewpoint (B2): Zossen: Soviet Memorial

Directions: Head out of Wünsdorf in a north westerly direction until you join the Berliner Chaussee/B96. Continue along B96 until you turn left off Strasse der Jugend onto Baruther Strasse, the memorial then comes up on your right. For satnav users, enter the nearest address, which is Baruther Strasse, 14, Zossen, Germany.

Zossen, like most other places in Brandenburg, was originally a Slavic settlement in the area of Lower Lusatia. It was classed as a Wendish townlet, whose small population made their living from working the swampy and sandy soil. Zossen later come under the administration of Brandenburg, and around 1568, Joachim II set about making the River Notte navigable. The electorates of Saxony and Brandenburg continued to contest the area over the next 250 years. It was not until 1815 that the area came under the permanent administration of Brandenburg. The coming of the railways in 1841 paved the way for rapid economic development. During the twentieth century, significant military projects altered the character of the area. It was not until the last Russian troops left in 1994 that the area was finally demilitarised. Since 2003,

Zossen air raid shelter.

Indian prisoners of war at Zossen during the First World War.

Zossen has consisted of a grouping of sixteen districts and municipalities, which now make up the town area. In recent years, the town has developed something of a reputation as being a hotbed of far-right extremism. In May 2015, local police arrested two suspects following an attempted arson attack on a refugee centre in nearby Wünsdorf. Despite the area's reputation, the author has always found site visits to be a tranquil and pleasant experience.

8

'Who is going to take Berlin?'

On 29 March, Zhukov flew to Moscow for preliminary discussions on the Berlin operation with Stalin. Konev arrived two days later, carrying with him his own plans for the assault on Hitler's capital. On 1 April, the *Stavka* met to finalise plans and preparations for the mighty blow, which was to crush Nazi Germany once and for all. As was his style, Stalin got down to business without any preamble by stating that he had received information, which indicated that, 'The little allies intend to get to Berlin before the Red Army.' Just so there would be no doubt, Stalin bade General Shtemenko to read the telegram from the Soviet mission to Eisenhower's headquarters, which appeared to confirm the 'less than allied' intentions of the British and Americans. Turning to Zhukov and Konev, Stalin asked, 'Well, now, who is going to take Berlin? We or the Allies?'

The question posed by Stalin was purely tactical and Konev was first to rise to the bait by replying, 'It is we who will be taking Berlin, and we shall take it before the Allies.' Stalin probed Konev by asking, 'How will you be able to organise a proper strike group for it? Your main forces are on your southern flank. Wouldn't you have to do a lot of redeployment?' Konev had spoken too quickly without having thought through the proposition. He assured Stalin that the necessary redeployments would be carried out in time. Stalin nodded his acceptance of Konev's assurances and then turned to Zhukov, who replied confidently, 'With respect, the men of the First Belorussian Front do not need any regrouping. They are ready now. We are aimed directly at Berlin. We are the nearest to Berlin. We shall take Berlin.' Stalin's tactic of playing off his marshals against each other was working well.

General Antonov went on to present the main operational plan, which aimed at piercing the German front in several places, isolating and destroying the main defensive forces, seizing Berlin and effecting a link up with Allied forces on the Elbe. The urgency of the situation left very little time for

Soviet artillery on the Oder.

planning the assault on Berlin, as operations were to commence no later than 16 April. Stalin ordered Zhukov and Konev to remain in Moscow and prepare their Front plans for final approval on 3 April. Zhukov's plan called for three simultaneous attacks on an 88-kilometre front stretching from the Hohenzollern Canal to the Oder-Spree rivers. The main attack would be launched by five armies from the bridgehead on the western bank of the Oder near Kustrin. On reaching Berlin's eastern approaches, the tank forces were to envelop the city by manoeuvring to the north and south. Two supporting attacks would aim at closing the envelopment. A thrust by two armies south of the Finow Canal would provide flank cover in the north while Rokossovsky's Front was completing its redeployments. An additional attack by two armies aimed at Brandenburg would complete the envelopment of Berlin and isolate the bulk of the German 9th Army. Konev planned two thrusts, the first aimed at Spremberg was to be carried out by two tank armies and three infantry armies crossing the Neisse between Forst and Muskau. The second would be launched from the Görlitz area and would aim to close in on the Elbe at Dresden.

Both plans were agreed without hesitation by Stalin. The only thing left to be decided was the boundary between the operational areas of each front. This was a somewhat tricky subject as back in November 1944, Stalin had promised Zhukov that his Front would have the honour of taking Berlin. However, for some time the planning staff had grappled with the thorny problem of co-ordinating the operations of the two Fronts. The demarcation line drawn on the operation map by the planning staff, which ran from the Neisse to

Potsdam effectively excluded Konev's Front from having any opportunity to aim for the main prize. With this in mind, Konev argued his case for having greater freedom of action. Stalin considered the problem and decided to adopt an Alexandrian solution by simply redrawing the demarcation line to a point that extended only as far as Lubben. He then announced: 'In the event of stiff enemy resistance on the eastern approaches to Berlin and the possible delay of the First Belorussian Front's offensive, the First Ukranian Front will be ready to deliver a blow from the south.' Subsequently, he gave a more precise expression of his intentions to initiate a contest between his marshals by saying, 'Whoever breaks in first, let him take Berlin.' The race for Berlin was on.

Zhukov and Konev flew out of Moscow within minutes of each other, such was their keen desire to make the most of every available moment. Zhukov had already contacted his Chief of Staff to inform him that the operational plan had been accepted more or less without alteration. Reconnaissance flights revealed the full extent of the formidable obstacle presented by the defences on the approaches to Berlin. Back in February, when Zhukov's troops had established their bridgeheads, there was no organised resistance between the Oder and Berlin. By April, the Germans had reinforced this vital sector, General Chuikov noted:

> The Nazis had established themselves particularly firmly on the banks of the Oder and the Neisse from Schwedt to Görlitz; the total depth of their natural and engineered defence lines reached thirty to forty kilometres. Most strongly fortified of all were the eastern approaches to Berlin, facing the line of advance of 1st Byelorussian Front. Here the depth of the prepared defences reached all the way from the Oder to the Berlin fortified area. During February, March and the first half of April the enemy had built up large forces in the Berlin direction. To the rear of the defence area there were strong reserves of motorised and panzer divisions which had been transferred from the western front. Up to one-half of all the enemy forces and means of support in the Berlin grouping were concentrated against the 1st Byelorussian Front, especially against the Oder bridgeheads held by the 5th Shock Army and the 8th Guards Army.

Zhukov elected for a frontal attack against the first German defensive belt dug in on the floor of the Oderbruch. He reasoned that the momentum of the assault would then carry the attacking troops forward on to the main German defence line sited on the Seelow Heights. His decision to launch a frontal attack against well-prepared defensive positions was a clear sign of his desire to beat Konev in the race to the Reichstag by taking the shortest possible route to Berlin. Final attack preparations consisting of special briefings and exercises were undertaken from 5–7 April, and then from 8–14 April.

Zhukov's main concern was how to utilise the enormous combat power at his disposal in order to achieve the maximum shock and awe effect on the enemy. He decided on a pre-dawn attack on a battlefield illuminated by 143 searchlights (which would provide artificial moonlight and, in theory, blind the enemy). The other question on which Zhukov pondered was how best to employ his two tank armies. At this point, it would be useful to look at the section of Zhukov's memoirs detailing his pre-attack deliberations concerning the use of tank forces *in extensio*:

> The question of using the tank armies was seriously discussed during the exercises when the breaching of the enemy tactical defences on the Oder was rehearsed. It was decided to commit the tank armies to battle only after the Seelow Heights were captured, on account of the strong tactical defences on these Seelow Heights. Naturally, we did not count on our tank armies gaining an opportunity for operational manoeuvring after the breaching of the tactical defences as had been the case, for example, in the previous Vistula-Oder, East Pomeranian and other operations. In the latter operations the tank armies had moved far ahead and created all conditions for the rapid movement forward by the field armies ... This was not envisaged in this operation, because the distance to Berlin along a straight line was not more than 60–80 kilometres. Therefore, the following was provided for. If the strength of the attack by the Front's first echelon was to prove insufficient to rapidly overcome the enemy tactical defences and the possibility of a delay was to arise, then both tank armies would be committed to smash the enemy defence. This would reinforce the attack of the infantry armies and help complete the breakthrough of the enemy tactical defences in the Oder and Seelow Heights area.

Having considered the possibility of being held up by strong enemy defences on the Seelow Heights, Zhukov amended the *Stavka* plan by deploying the 1st Guards Tank Army directly behind the infantry of the 8th Guards Army. This contingency meant that both armies could attack together should the need arise. It was a messy solution to a difficult problem. All Stalin could do in the situation was agree by saying, 'Do as you think best, you're in a better position to judge on the spot.' On the day, Stalin's agreement to Zhukov's solution would later lead to dramatic and almost disastrous consequences.

On 14 April, Zhukov launched a reconnaissance in force along the 40-kilometre frontage of his planned main assault. Supported by tanks and artillery, battalion strength groups probed the forward German positions covering the Seelow Heights and in some places achieved penetrations of 5 kilometres. In his memoirs, Zhukov describes how the aggressive probing forced German units to reveal their positions prematurely:

A searchlight at Seelow Soviet memorial and cemetery.

> The enemy mistook the reconnaissance for the beginning of our offensive. Suffice it to say that some German units were dislodged from their forward positions as a result of action by our recon groups, and almost the entire German artillery took part in repelling the recon group attacks. The aim we had pursued had been attained. The enemy rushed his reserves to the second positions. However, our troops stopped their advance and dug in. This was perplexing for the enemy command. As it was learned later, some of the German commanders decided that our offensive had failed.

As can be seen, Zhukov gives the impression that his aggressive probe succeeded in fooling the Germans into thinking that it was his main assault. However, Zhukov's somewhat tainted memoirs need to be treated with caution. Heinrici was an old hand who understood Soviet offensive doctrine. His post-war study of the battle contradicts Zhukov's assertion that the German command had been completely fooled:

> On 14 April the enemy continued with the attack, but now he did not restrict himself to the front northwest of Kustrin, but extended it to the full width of his bridgehead and expanded in the south up to Lebus. On the northern flank the enemy got as far as Eichwerder, five kilometres southeast from Wriezen. By doing this his bridgehead had reached a width of approximately fifteen kilometres. West of Kustrin he got to the Hauptgraben Canal, that is, to the line of defence that according to the plans should be occupied by the 9. *Armee* ... Despite the fact the Russians had broadened their attack that day, the German command believed that this assault was only a preparatory attack like those the Russians used to carry out before every battle. One reason for this assumption was the limitation of the zone of attack, the other the nature of the fight, which was already starting to fade away during the midday hours and obviously had not been conducted with the full employment of all arms and ammunition of the enemy.

Heinrici's belief that the main attack was imminent was supported by a second day of localised attacks, which further probed his defences. These attacks revealed the German front line to be fully manned. By the evening of 15 April, Heinrici had sufficient evidence to judge exactly when the main blow would fall. After carefully weighing up the situation, he turned to his aides and said, 'I believe the attack will take place in the early hours tomorrow. Move back and take up positions on the second line of defence.' As dark came, the bulk of the troops moved back, leaving only a skeleton force behind. Knowing that the Soviet's always preceded their main attacks with a heavy bombardment, Heinrici aimed to ride the first blow by ensuring that the vast weight of hot steel unleashed by Zhukov would fall on empty ground.

The night of 15–16 April dragged on interminably, being enlivened only by sporadic German artillery fire. Searchlights and flares dropped from aircraft lit up the areas where Zhukov's forces were massing. However, from the Soviet side of the hill, all remained quiet as the artillery was under strict instructions to hold fire until the appointed time. At approximately 1 a.m. (German time), Zhukov arrived at Chuikov's field headquarters located on Hill 81.5 near Reitwein. According to Chuikov, his presence was not altogether welcome:

> Unexpectedly, the observation post of the Front Commander was also transferred here. Frankly speaking many officers, including myself, did not particularly welcome the presence of superior officers at their command and observation posts; it was easier to control the course of an action without them. Higher authorities like to interfere, and do not always make the happiest corrections of their subordinate's decisions; in the presence of a senior officer one has a matter of propriety to inform him of what decisions one proposes to take, and he may not approve them, which fetters initiative.

These words may form part of Chiukov's post-war attempts to characterise Zhukov as an interfering bungler, as such they need to be treated with caution. Therefore, it is worthwhile to contrast this account with Zhukov's own in which he describes his arrival at Chuikov's headquarters:

> Late at night, a few hours before the artillery and air barrage, I set out for the observation post of 8th Guards Army Commander General Chuikov. Along the way I managed to meet many commanders of rifle and tank units and the 1st Guards Tank Army Commander, General Katukov, and his Chief of Staff, General Shalin ... I could only marvel at our tank-men, how they had raised their operational and tactical skills during the war. It was in such high spirits that I arrived together with Member of the Military Council K. F. Telegin and Front Artillery Commander V.I. Kazakov at the observation post of 8th Guards Army Commander Chuikov ... It was 3 a.m. Moscow time. Last-minute checks of combat readiness for the operation were being made in all the units. Everything was done efficiently, calmly, and at the same time without unwarranted self-assurance and underestimation of the enemy... The checks were completed in an hour and a half. Artillery barrage was fixed for 5 a.m. Moscow time. The hands of the clock moved slowly as never before. In order to fill the remaining minutes we decided to have some hot strong tea which was made for us by a girl. I remember that she had a non-Russian name, Margot. We sipped tea in silence, each deep in his thoughts.

The tension during those last few minutes was palpable as Zhukov and Chuikov emerged from their dugout to take their places at the specially constructed observation post. In the jumping off areas men and machines were poised for the great breakthrough, which would take them to Berlin.

At 3 a.m. (German time), three red flares shot up into the sky signalling the start of the attack. Then, the massed artillery struck, 6,464 guns, and 1,078 rocket launchers unleashed a storm of fire, the like of which had never been experienced before. With a density of 400 guns per 1.5 kilometres, the bombardment succeeded in dumping over 500,000 shells, rockets and mortar bombs on the German positions up to a depth of 8.5 kilometres. In the sky, bombers and ground attack aircraft added their weight to the opening barrage. It seemed that no living thing could survive such an onslaught. Zhukov was convinced that the barrage had cleared the enemy, later stating in his memoirs:

> A few bursts of machine gun fire were heard from the enemy side in the first seconds, and then everything quietened down. It seemed as if there were not a single living creature left on the enemy side. The enemy did not make a single shot during the thirty-minute powerful artillery barrage. This showed that the enemy was completely suppressed and the defence system disrupted.

> For this reason it was decided to shorten the time of the artillery preparation and immediately begin the general offensive. Thousands of flares of different colour flew into the air. This was the signal for 140 searchlights placed at intervals of 200 metres to flash spot lights equalling more than 100,000 million candlepower, lighting up the battlefield and blinding the enemy and snatching objects for attack by our tanks and infantry from the darkness. It was a striking picture, and I remember having seen nothing like it during my whole life!

Zhukov's recollections of this phase of the attack do not bear scrutiny. His opening barrage fell on largely empty positions. Moreover, his intention of blinding the German defenders with horizontally directed beams of light was nothing short of a fiasco. The searchlights failed to penetrate the dense smoke and dust created by the barrage. Advancing troops found themselves silhouetted for the benefit of the enemy.

Already unnerved, their situation was further compounded by the countermanding of orders given by front line officers to turn the searchlights off. As the searchlights were turned on and off, troops lost their night vision and became increasingly disorientated.

From his viewpoint on Hill 81.5, Zhukov could see virtually nothing and as a consequence was disconnected from the chaotic events unfolding on the battlefield. He remained oblivious to the immense difficulties his advance units were encountering as they attempted to negotiate the sodden, soggy morass at the base of the Seelow Heights. His growing irritation at the lack of progress developed into rage by midday following the failure of Chuikov's 8th Guards Army to advance beyond the third line of German defences on the Hauptgraben Canal. Chuikov had already issued orders for a renewed infantry assault aimed at the capture of Seelow, Friedersdorf, and Dolgelin. The assault was due to go in at 2 p.m.; however, Zhukov decided that he could not wait and so decided to smash his way through to the heights with his main tank forces. Chuikov later wrote in scathing terms about this rash decision:

> The Front Commander, who was present at my observation post, decided to speed up the process of breaking through and seizing positions on the Seelow Heights, by throwing into battle Katukov's 1st Mechanised Army. I requested him not to do this, since our Army had sufficient forces to carry out the assignment given it, and proposed that the general plan of the offensive should not be interfered with, but carried through systematically. I considered that, until the Army had scaled the Seelow Heights, tank formations should not be brought into the battle; they would not perform the task, would not speed up the rate of advance. But Marshal Zhukov was not fond of withdrawing orders once given.

Information board on the Reitwein Spur.

Und das Zielen?
Auge, Kimme der Visieröffnung für die jeweilige Entfernung (50, 100, 150 m), Korn am Geschoßkopf und Ziel müssen eine Linie bilden (genau wie Kimme und Korn beim Gewehr). Am besten hältst Du auf Mitte Panzer (Unterkante Turm). Im übrigen beachte: Bergauf, gegen Wind — höherhalten; bergab, mit Wind tieferhalten. Damit Du auch bei schlechter Beleuchtung schießen kannst, sind Kimme und Korn mit Leuchtfarbe bestrichen. Je besser Du die Entfernung schätzt, um so sicherer wirst Du den Panzer treffen.

Motto:

> Nicht das Schießen tut's alleine,
> Auch Entfernung spricht für sich,
> Willst Du Panzer treffen,
> So verschätz' Dich nicht!

Achte besonders auf dies:
Kommst Du nicht zum Schuß, vergiß nicht die Panzerfaust wieder zu sichern.
Blindgänger nicht anfassen! Liegen lassen, wenn möglich, sprengen. Zündvergaser können vorkommen, dann nicht an der Panzerfaust herumdoktern, dazu ist sie zu gefährlich. Weglegen, später sprengen.

Eine Bitte noch in Deinem eigenen Interesse!
Sorge nach Möglichkeit dafür, daß die abgeschossenen Rohre nach hinten kommen. Die Heimat braucht sie, um Dir eine neue Panzerfaust zu schicken. Außerdem sind Prämien für die Rückgabe ausgesetzt.

Und nun: Panzerknacker-Heil!

4000000. 1. 45. (B) M 0/601

Pzf — 100 m | D 560/4

Die Panzerfaust

Die Panzerfaust ist D e i n e Pak! Du kannst mit ihr jeden Panzer bis auf Höchstentfernungen von 150 m abschießen. Je näher Du ihn aber herankommen läßt, um so sicherer erledigst Du ihn. Lies Dir dies Merkblatt richtig durch, dann kann Dir, wenn es darauf ankommt, nichts passieren.

Wie sieht die Panzerfaust - 100 m aus?

Der Kopf enthält eine H-Ladung, die jeden zur Zeit bekannten Feindpanzer durchschlägt, auch an der dicksten

German *Panzerfaust* instruction leaflet. (*Author's collection*)

Napoleon once said, 'The battlefield is a scene of constant chaos. The winner will be the one who controls the chaos, both his own and the enemies.' Zhukov was either unaware of this maxim or chose to ignore it, as he added to, rather than controlled the chaotic situation pertaining on the battlefield. The premature commitment of his tank forces resulted in jamming the few roads open for movement, which in turn hindered the passage of artillery needed for the infantry assault on the heights. Only on the right flank was any progress made as Soviet armour drew up to the town of Seelow. However, the tanks proved easy meat for well sited 88-mm guns and *Panzerfaust* teams. By midnight, three houses in the northern part of Seelow had been captured. However, no breakthrough was in sight.

To the south, Konev's operation was progressing much more smoothly. The opening bombardment, which commenced at 4.15 a.m. (German time) was more effective than Zhukov's opening salvo as the flat trajectory fire served to subdue the German defenders. The laying down of a dense smoke screen enabled the first wave to cross the Neisse with little opposition. They were followed by a second wave carrying bridging equipment. Within twenty minutes of the first crossing, a small bridgehead had been consolidated. An hour later, the first of Konev's armour, which had been ferried across the river, was already in action. By this time, 133 of the planned 150 river crossings between Forst and Muskau had been secured. By 9 a.m., the first bridges capable of supporting heavy armour were being laid. Two hours later, the lead brigades of General Lelushenko's 4th Tank Army were in action on the west bank. They were under instruction to forge ahead to the Spree and then ford the river. By the following day, Konev's forces were half-way to Cottbus. Meanwhile, Zhukov's troops were still floundering in the killing field chosen by Heinrici as his main line of defence.

Heinrici could look back on the outcome of the first day's fighting with a degree of relief. General Busse's 9th Army had taken the full force of Zhukov's attack, but was still holding out everywhere. In the Frankfurt-an-der-Oder sector local counterattacks had even succeeded in throwing the enemy back. The daily brief to the High Command reads:

> Along the front of the 9. *Armee* the Soviets launched their expected major attack. The attack was supported by a two and a half hour heavy barrage from 2,500 artillery pieces and 1,600 mortars with an ammunition expenditure of approximately 450,000 shells. In addition the attack was supported by 2,000 aircraft and the employment of approximately 450 tanks ... The courageously fighting German divisions succeeded in preventing a Soviet breakthrough during the heavy fighting. The hard fighting was marked by the destruction of 150 Soviet tanks and 132 Soviet aircraft ... Through the employment of all local reserves a large number of

> Soviet breakthroughs were blocked and partially retaken ... In the southern area of the main effort, south of Fortress Frankfurt, the enemy could only be stopped by employment of all available reserves in a weak isolated front and partly thrown back in counter attacks. North of Frankfurt the troops put up a tough defence in Mallnow and led decisive counter attacks against an enemy supported by fifty tanks, achieving a successful defence.

The remarkable results achieved by Busse's 9th Army prompted Guderian's successor, General Krebs, to congratulate Heinrici by saying, 'Well, we have all good reason to feel satisfied.' Heinrici conceded that there was some cause for satisfaction by replying, 'Considering the size of the attack we have not lost much ground.' His less than enthusiastic response betrayed the grim truth that his forces were massively outnumbered and that they could not hope to stave off defeat for much longer. In his post-war study, Heinrici summarised the outcome of the opening day of Zhukov's offensive:

> All-in-all by the evening of 16 April the outcome of the first day of the major attack did not seem to be too unsatisfactory, if one compared the weakness of the defence on the river with the superiority of the Russian attack. At least the enemy had not attained a breakthrough on this day.

Heinrici's cautious optimism was based on his assessment of the real conditions pertaining on the battlefront. His troops had only enough ammunition for two and a half days of combat. There were chronic shortages of men and materiel everywhere and signs of disintegration were beginning to appear. In the crucial Seelow Heights sector, General Helmuth Weidling's 56th Panzer Corps was continuing to cover all possible approaches, but its formations, particularly the brittle 9th Parachute Division, could not be expected to hold for long. Speaking to his staff late in the evening, Heinrici summed up his thoughts on the inevitable outcome of the unequal struggle by saying, 'They cannot hold much longer. The men are so exhausted that their tongues are hanging out.' The following day would bring more heavy fighting and increased strain on Heinrici's hard pressed forces.

The attack resumed at dawn along the entire length of the front held by the 9th Army. In the Seelow sector, the 56th Panzer Corps continued to take a heavy toll of Soviet armour and infantry. However, as the day wore on, numbers began to tell and the defence of the crucial heights began to give way. The tactical situation forced Heinrici into the piecemeal introduction of his limited reserves. Consequently, they were not able to form a unified barrier with which to blunt the Soviet advance. By midday, the 1st Rifle Battalion of the 172nd Regiment of the 8th Guards Army commanded by Captain Nikolai Chusovskoi had broken into the south western outskirts of Seelow. Fierce fighting ensued in which two German self-propelled guns, one tank, a mortar battery, and twelve firing points were put out of action. By nightfall, Seelow had fallen to Chuikov's troops, but the heights remained in German hands. To the south, Konev's forces were continuing to advance towards Cottbus, threatening the right flank of the 9th Army.

On the third day of the battle, Zhukov's forces succeeded in forcing deep penetrations from north and south of Seelow towards Marxdorf and Müncheberg. Counterattacks by German reserve units met with little success as they were brushed aside. The 18th *Panzergrenadier* Division and the 11th SS *Panzergrenadier* Division Nordland were pushed westwards to Berlin. Meanwhile, the 23rd SS *Panzergrenadier* Division Nederland was being pushed southwards towards the northern flank of the 9th Army. The inevitable major breakthrough came on the following day, when the daily brief to the German High Command noted:

> A further deterioration of the situation in the major defensive battle of the 9.*Armee* occurred yesterday along the point of main effort in the areas of Müncheberg and Wriezen. The battle stands at a point of decision ... In heavy defensive fighting it was reported by messages that 226 enemy tanks were destroyed.

By the end of the day, the tactical situation remained somewhat vague, questioning whether this was, indeed, the point of decision as far as the battle was concerned. Zhukov certainly thought so, as in his memoirs he singles out this day as the day in which the decisive breakthrough was made: 'Only on April 19, having sustained heavy losses the Germans gave in to the mighty onslaught of our tank and infantry armies and began to retire to the outer perimeter of the Berlin defence area.' Zhukov's assessment of the situation is essentially correct as by the end of the day the German defensive front had all but collapsed. Remnants of the 9th Army and the 4th Panzer Army faced envelopment by Zhukov's forces. Further danger lay in the form of those elements of Konev's Front, which had broken through in the south. These forces were now heading northwards in the direction of Zossen.

On 20 April, Weidling's 56th Panzer Corps continued to be subjected to heavy attacks. An assault on Dahmsdorf was repelled, but Müncheberg and the villages of Hasenholz, Ruhlsdorf, and Klosterdorf were all captured during the course of the day. The afternoon report to the High Command outlined the deteriorating situation:

> The 1st Guards Tank Army has pierced our front in the area of the Frankfurt—Berlin *Autobahn* and *Reichsbahn 1* Kustrin—Berlin by leaving behind its infantry and covering this breakthrough by thrusts to the south

Seelow Soviet memorial.

Soviet graves at Seelow.

> and southeast. The 2nd Guards Tank Army succeeded in tearing up the forces of the *LV1. Pz* and *CL. Korps* and in breaking through in the sector Strausberg—Bernau and in reaching the Greater Berlin outer defence area.

The loss of Müncheberg brought an end to the defence of the eastern approaches to Berlin. Weidling's 56th Panzer Corps was being pushed further and further back. Meanwhile, Busse's extended front, anchored around Frankfurt-an-der-Oder was rapidly crumbling. For Army Group Vistula, time was fast running out.

9

Tour C: Seelow–Manschnow–Reitwein

Viewpoint (C1): Seelow: 20th *Panzergrenadier* Memorial and War Graves

Directions: From your Berlin base, take the B1 via Müncheberg to Seelow. Continue onto Diedersdorfer Strasse and then follow the road until you see the Lidl Store coming up on your left. Take the next left onto Gorlsdorfer Weg, the graves and memorial come up on your immediate right opposite the Lidl store. For satnav users, enter Gorlsdorfer Weg, 3, Seelow, Germany.

The 20th *Panzergrenadier* Division was originally formed in 1934 under the cover name *Reichswehr Dienstelle Hamburg*. In March 1935, Hitler announced the re-introduction of conscription and the creation of a thirty-six division-strong Army, which would henceforth be a branch of the Wehrmacht (Armed Forces). Shortly afterwards, the cover name was dropped and the unit took on its official title of the 20th Infantry Division. In October, the division was upgraded and became known as the 20th Motorised Infantry Division. The division later took part in the campaigns in Poland and France. In June 1941, it took part in the invasion of the Soviet Union under Army Group Centre. In September, it was transferred to Army Group North, where it saw action on the Leningrad Front. In December 1942, it was transferred to Army Group South in order join other forces in a relief effort aimed at extricating German troops trapped in Velikiye Luki. In July 1943, the division was equipped with an assault gun battalion and was subsequently redesignated as the 20th *Panzergrenadier* Division. It remained on the Eastern Front for the remainder of the war, frequently taking on a 'fire brigade' role in emergency situations.

On 27 March 1945, the division took part in a failed attempt to relieve Kustrin. As part of Weidling's 56th Panzer Corps, it was pushed back into

Berlin. The divisional commander *Generalmajor* Georg Scholze committed suicide in Potsdam on 23 April. Nine days previously, his wife and four of his children were killed in an Allied bombing raid. The division was surrounded and largely destroyed in the Battle of Berlin. On the fiftieth anniversary of the battle in 1995, the Old Comrades Association of the division erected the memorial, which now stands in the cemetery grounds in Seelow. A rough translation of the inscription on the memorial reads, 'Unforgotten, dedicated to the fallen and missed comrades who in and around Seelow lost their lives in 1945. Donated by the former comrades 76th—20th Pz Gren Div Hamburg. Pray for peace.'

To the left of the memorial is an individual grave named to Major Rudolf Ihde, who, as commander of Storm Regiment 195, received the Knights Cross on 23 September 1943. There are a further ten named military graves in the cemetery out of an overall total of 649 burials.

History

Seelow is first mentioned in 1252 in the records kept by Archbishop Wilbrand of Magdeburg. He often found himself in conflict with the Ascanian Lords (House of Anhalt) whose territorial ambitions resulted in a series of gains for Brandenburg at the expense of Magdeburg. The Brandenburg Ascanian line died out in 1320. The dynasty continued in the Saxon state of Saxe-Wittenberg until 1422 and the state of Saxe-Lauenburg until 1689. Ascanians continued to rule in the small state of Anhalt until the dissolution of the monarchy in 1918.

The town suffered major fires in 1630, 1788, and 1809, but recovered to become the administrative hub of the Lebus district following the relocation of the district council offices in 1863. In 1950, the area was renamed 'Seelow District' following boundary changes agreed in 1945. Seelow retained its status as an administrative centre until 1993. In 2001, the town was granted a coat of arms, the design being based upon the earliest known town seal dating back to 1429. You will see examples of the coat of arms, which consist of a blue shield with two boat hooks and a mitre symbolising St Adalbert of Prague who was murdered by fishermen while undertaking missionary duties in the area.

Viewpoint (C2): Seelow: The Seelow Heights Museum

Directions: Head east up Gorlsdorfer Weg towards the town, then turn left onto Berliner Strasse. Follow the road to the roundabout continue onto Kustriner Strasse. Follow the road crossing a small brick built bridge which carries you over the rail tracks. The museum then comes up on your right. There is usually plenty of parking space available. For satnav users, enter Kustriner Strasse, 28, Seelow, Germany.

Seelow *Panzergrenadier* memorial.

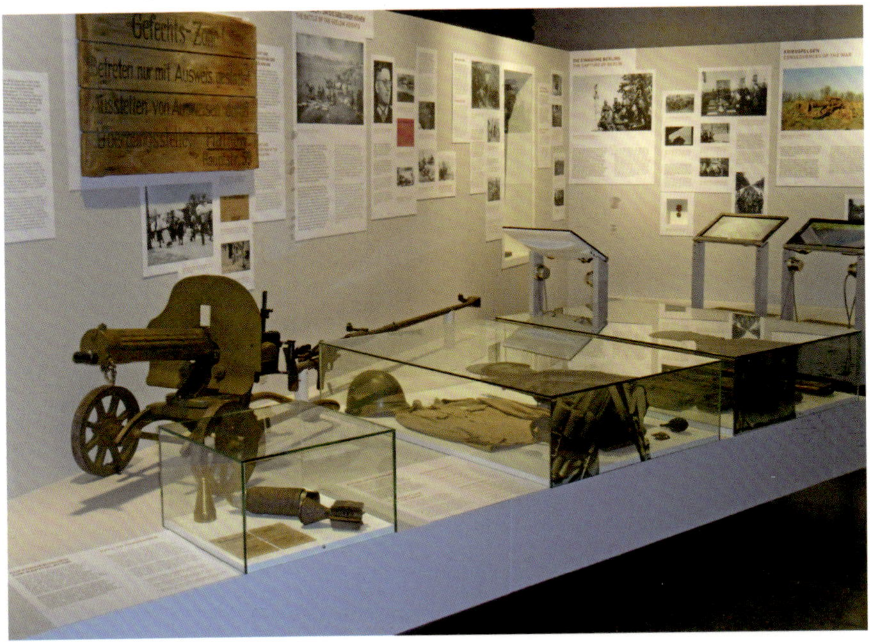

The interior of the Seelow Heights Museum.

The Seelow Heights Museum opened in 1972. The style is based on a typical Red Army bunker of the period and symbolises the close ties between East Germany and the Soviet Union. Since unification, that emphasis has changed; consequently, the museum now looks at the conflict more objectively. The small but first-rate display provides some valuable insights into those final battles for the eastern approaches to Berlin. There is a cinema, which shows an English language film about the site (I would suggest that you only watch the film if you are not pushed for time as it lasts for a good thirty minutes). Also on site, you will find a small selection of books (mostly in German) and keenly priced souvenir items.

The Seelow monument and military cemetery is located to the rear of the museum. Upon leaving the museum, take the steps on your left and make your way to the higher level behind. On your left, you will see the cemetery, which is reserved for sixty-nine receipients of the award of 'Hero of the Soviet Union.' Interestingly, only the relatives of party members were given notification of the death in action of their loved ones. As such, there was usually a rush of applications to join the party before any major action. On the night of 15 April, the eve of the Seelow assault, 2,000 officers and men applied for membership of the Communist Party. During the lull from February to April, approximately 17,000 officers and men became party members.

Opposite the cemetery, you will see the Seelow memorial designed by Lev Kerbel and Vladimir Zigal. The centrepiece of the memorial is a bronze sculpture depicting a victorious member of the Red Army standing triumphantly besides the turret of a destroyed German panzer.

The memorial was inaugurated on 27 November 1945. The inscription on the base reads, 'Eternal fame for the heroes who fell fighting the Fascist invaders for the freedom and independence of the Soviet Union.' Kerbel and Zigal were also responsible for creating the Tiergarten memorial on Strasse des 17 Juni in Berlin along with architect Nikolai Sergijevski. In 1977, a panel was installed on the Seelow memorial bearing the inscription:

> Soviet soldiers you will be remembered forever, chiselled in stone, the names endure, the deeds alive in our memory. You gave your lives to free us from Fascism and war; what burned inside you will remain a torch within us. What you hated, we will hate even more, what you loved, we will love deeply, the cause you died for, will be our reason for living.

The inscription was penned by German poet and author Helmut Preissler and follows a pattern in which the 'Fascists' bear sole responsibility for the war. It was against the backdrop of this monument that swearing-in ceremonies for the East German National People's Army took place.

Carry on walking past the memorial and you will come to a cast concrete relief map of the Seelow Heights battlefield. From here, you will get a fine view of the Oderbruch and the Reitwein Spur. This visit will have taken up most of the morning, and so if you are ready for a spot of lunch, I suggest heading to Seelow town square (Puschkinplatz). Here you will find several eateries (also snack vans on market days).

Viewpoint (C3): Manschnow: Soviet Cemetery

Directions: Head down the B1 in the direction of Kustrin (Kostrzyn). Turn right onto Lindenstrasse, then follow the road around to Ahornweg. Turn right onto Friedenstrasse, the church and cemetery will come up on your right just as you pass Kirchstrasse. For satnav users, enter Friedenstrasse, 45, Manschnow (Kustriner Vorland), Germany.

The Soviet Cemetery at Manschnow contains the remains of 1,200 officers and men. The large number of burials bears witness to the hard fighting, which took place as Chuikov's forces established a firm bridgehead on the line of Klessin–Podelzig–Hathenow–Rathstock–Manschnow–Kietz during early February.

Viewpoint (C4): Reitwein: Soviet Cemetery

Directions: Head down Kirschstrasse and then turn left onto Frankfurter Strasse/B112. Continue along B112 past Rathstock and then take the L331/Hauptstrasse to Reitwein. Turn right onto Zwingerweg, follow the road to the bottom and then turn left onto Hathenower Weg. The cemetery will then come up on your left. For satnav users, enter Hathenower Weg, 3, Reitwein, Germany.

The Soviet Cemetery in Reitwein is sited in the grounds of the former *Schloss* and faces the forested area leading to the spur where Zhukov commanded the attack on the Seelow Heights. There are approximately 3,000 burials on site, with the vast majority being unnamed. During the DDR period, a ceremony took place in February each year to commemorate the sacrifices made in capturing this strategically important position. An honour guard was provided by the garrison at Kustrin and students from the High School in Podelzig would lay wreaths. In 2008, the Cemetery and memorial underwent a restoration, which was funded by the government of the Russian Federation.

Reitwein Soviet cemetery.

The sign pointing the way to Zhukov's field HQ on the Reitwein Spur.

Viewpoint (C5): Reitwein: Marshal Zhukov Field HQ

> Directions: From the cemetery, turn to the right and walk up the track marked Shukow-Befehisstand, which takes you past some farm buildings and dwellings. As you walk up the path do not be too alarmed by the incessant barking of dogs, particularly that coming from the dwellings on your left. The dogs sound fierce, but they are securely fenced in and present no danger. Continue to follow the signposted path, which curves around to the left and then leads on into the forested area. Note the revetments for tanks and communication trenches as you continue to walk through the forest. Turning to your right, take the steps leading up to the restored entrance of the 8th Guards Army command post. It is not possible to enter the command post as the tunnels, which were originally created by blasts from flamethrowers (forming a terracotta effect), have long since collapsed.
>
> After having viewed the command post entrance, take the steps up the steep pathway (be especially careful in wet conditions). When you reach the top, follow the path to the restored observation post (for your own safety, I would suggest staying within the restored area).

Trees now largely obscure the view, but in autumn and winter, it is just about possible to see the Seelow Heights in the distance. It is worth noting the photograph on the information board, which shows Zhukov looking distinctly concerned. It was Moltke the Elder who said, 'No operation extends with any certainty beyond the first encounter with the main body of the enemy.' However, it would be true to say that Zhukov's plan began to unravel even before first contact with Heinrici's forces was made. Therefore, with Zhukov's poor handling of the Seelow Heights battle in mind, it is perhaps more appropriate to quote Clausewitz, who said:

> Everything is very simple in war, but the simplest thing is difficult. These difficulties accumulate and produce a friction, which no man can imagine exactly who has not seen war. Suppose now a traveller, who towards the evening, expects to accomplish the two stages at the end of his day's journey, four or five leagues, with post horses, on the high road—it is nothing. He arrives now at the last station but one, finds no horses, or very bad ones, then a hilly country, bad roads; it is a dark night, and he is glad when, after a great deal of trouble, he reaches the next station, and finds there some miserable accommodation. So in war, through the influence of an infinity of petty circumstances, which cannot properly be described on paper, things disappoint us, and we fall short of the mark. A powerful iron will overcome this friction, it crushes the obstacles, but certainly the machine along with them. We shall often meet with this result. Like an obelisk, towards which

> the principal streets of a place converge, the strong will of a proud spirit, stands prominent and commanding, in the middle of the act of war.

These words sum up Zhukov's situation perfectly. Under pressure from Stalin, he threw in his armour (the powerful iron) prematurely and while he eventually succeeded in crushing resistance on the heights, the cost in both men and machines was enormous.

If you wish to take a break before heading back to your Berlin base, you could call into the Hotel *Zum-Heiratsmarkt* (Triftweg, 3, Reitwein), which is open Friday—Sunday during the main tourist season (Monday–Thursday on request—Mr Kaiser: 0333601 3174). During the evenings, the venue hosts music and cabaret events (check website for details: zum-heiratsmarkt-reitwein.de); recent performers have included the 'Fox Street Allstars' (blues band) and 'Big Helga' (the mind boggles). The owner, *Herr* Kaiser, occasionally organises 'War Walks' around the Reitwein Spur area (see events listings on website for details).

History

Reitwein is first mentioned in a document dating back to 1316 that records the sale by the Margrave of Brandenburg, Waldemar the Great, of Ruthewyn (as the village was then known) to Jacob von Gummer and Johann Schyele. In 1414, the village was raised to the same status as Gusow and Platkow. In 1572, the village was bought by Caspar von Platen. Six years later, he began converting his farmstead into a country estate. The village was sold again in 1666, this time to Joachim Erdman von Burgsdorf who built an impressive manor house between 1697 and 1700. Frederick the Great used the manor for his headquarters before the Battle of Zorndorf in 1758. A year later, he would return following his defeat at the Battle of Kunersdorf. Extensive alterations were carried out to the manor and gardens following the marriage of Erdmuth Amaile von Burgsdorf to Count Rudolf von Finkenstein in 1842.

At the beginning of February 1945, Reitwein found itself in the front line. A scratch division had been formed to defend the critical triangle of Klessin–Wuhden–Podelzig against Soviet incursions. The division was commanded by *Generalmajor* Adolf Raegener who had been severely wounded on the Eastern Front in December 1943 and had more recently held command positions in the Pomeranian Lakeland region and at Fortress Kustrin. The miscellany of trained and half-trained forces at Raegener's disposal included the *Volkssturm* battalions Hessen and Potsdam, the replacement battalion Buddenberg (from the unit Feldherrnalle), a so-called Alarm battalion, a Labour Service battalion, and an SS Artillery training regiment.

Serving on Raegener's staff was the Squire of Reitwein, Lieutenant Colonel Curt von Wittich, who at the age of seventy-two had come out of retirement to defend his own locality. He took an infantry platoon from Podelzig to reinforce the Labour Service troops in Reitwein who had been pushed back to the manor following a surprise attack by the 6th Company of the 220th Guards Rifle Regiment on 2 February. The strategically important tip of the Reitwein Spur was captured on the following day. Within twenty-four hours, the remaining German defenders had been ejected from the spur. The German response was to attack the Soviet positions with Stukas and artillery.

The loss of the Reitwein Spur prompted Raegener to telephone SS General Friedrich Wilhelm Kruger on the civilian network to urgently request additional forces with which he could launch a counter-attack. The only combat-ready reserves available between Frankfurt/Oder and Kustrin were the 1st Battalion of the *Panzergrenadier* Regiment Kurmark and the 2nd Battalion of the Brandenburg Panzer Regiment. Both units were stationed to the south of Podelzig and were ordered to link up with Raegener's Buddenberg/ Feldherrnalle battalion and other *ad hoc* units for the attack, which was due to go in at 5 p.m. The order from Raegener to the Alarm battalion and the Buddenberg/Feldherrnalle battalion stated:

> Battalion 'Feldherrnalle' will attack across the road from Wuhden to Reitwein. The *Alarm Bataillon* will attack the enemy on the Reitwein Spur along the Podelzig to Reitwein Road and will initially take Reitwein. The majority of *II./Panzer Regiment 'Brandenburg'* (*Panther Abteilung*) will advance across the road from Podelzig to Hathenow as far as the brickyard, turn east, and with the *Alarm Bataillon* and the Bataillon 'Feldherrnalle' take the village of Reitwein.

Further orders went out to the Kurmark *Panzergrenadiers* who would isolate the Görlitz crossing and push the Soviet troops back across the Oder.

A complete lack of communications equipment resulted in a poorly coordinated attack, which failed to dislodge the Soviets from their positions on the Reitwein Spur. Recognising the importance of the area, reinforcements including strong anti-tank elements had been drafted in to ward off the expected German riposte. The Buddenberg/Feldherrnalle battalion attacked in a north-easterly direction, but were forced to dig in 500 meters north of Wuhden. The Alarm battalion and *ad hoc* units were stopped by determined Soviet resistance near the tip of the Reitwein Spur. The attack by Brandenburg's Panther tanks was halted on the edge of Reitwein by strong anti-tank defences. The Kurmark Battalion initially made good progress until they encountered an infantry battalion backed up by artillery close to the heavily defended crossing point opposite Görlitz. The Soviet troops succeeded in stopping Kurmark in

Volkssturm recruiting poster: 'For freedom and life'. (*Author's collection*)

Battle zone: permits required notice.

its tracks; they then launched a flanking attack of their own towards Klessin. Fierce close-quarter fighting took place in Klessin on the following day. The village was held, albeit at heavy cost. That day, a further attempt to eliminate the Soviet lodgements failed. Both sides continued to contest the strategically important Reitwein Spur; in the process, Lebus, along with the villages of Klessin, Wuhden, Podelzig, and Mallnow became victims of the fierce struggle for supremacy on the battlefield.

The area took years to recover after the war. In 1947, the Oder flooded, resulting in extensive damage, which reached as far as Bad Freienwalde. Approximately 20,000 people were left homeless. During the DDR period, Reitwein was an agricultural area. The manor, which had survived the fighting in 1945 relatively intact, was demolished in 1962. All that now remains is a hedge marking the outline of the building along with a marker stone and some information boards (located between Zwingerweg and Hauptstrasse). During the post-unification period, Reitwein has benefited from the abolishment of the collective-farm system. Some dispossessed landowners returned, including the descendants of the former squire who took up residence in 1993.

10

Breakwaters

While Zhukov's opening attack on 16 April descended into chaos, Konev's forces made rapid headway against more fragmented opposition. By 18 April, the 4th Panzer Army had fallen back on Cottbus and Spremberg. Konev's *modus operandi* was to avoid centres of resistance whenever possible and press on. His formations bypassed Spremberg on 20 April, leaving behind a pocket of German troops, which included elements of the 10th SS Panzer Division *Frundsberg*, the *Führer* Escort Division, and the 344th Infantry Division. The divisional commanders received the usual 'last man, last bullet' orders that were as uncompromising as they were nonsensical:

> The gap in the front existing in your sector between Spremberg and Cottbus is to be closed by immediate attacks to the north. You are held personally responsible for completion of these orders. You must carry out the attack to victory or fall with your Division.

The divisional commanders reached the conclusion that the attack orders were unrealistic, if not downright suicidal. They therefore decided to ignore the orders and instead break out and join the bulk of Busse's 9th Army, which had been pushed to the south of Berlin. A vivid account of the breakout is provided by *Oberleutnant* Arnold of the *Führer* Escort Division. The account reads:

> Before us several hundred grenadiers, armoured troop carriers, and tanks had already set off across the meadow. Mortar shells fell among them and among the vehicles. Several tanks and armoured troop carriers were already burning ... Dead lay strewn all around. Wounded staggered, screaming; more and more vehicles were knocked out, human bodies whirled through the air, shattered, burned ... The entire meadow was littered with dead, wounded and burning combat vehicles. An armoured troop carrier carrying women

> and children was hit. Bodies whirled through the air. I ran on...In front of me, someone fell in the tracer fire from a burst of machine-gun fire. He pulled his pistol from its holster, placed it against his forehead and collapsed...Through the smoke I saw General Jolasse beside me trying to jump onto an armoured troop carrier that was overtaking us. He failed; he slid and fell, got up again and hurried on.

As Arnold's account graphically shows, the *Führer* Escort Division suffered particularly badly during the breakout. Only 400 troops from the division managed to successfully break through towards Dresden, where they were formed into a Battle Group. The fragmented *Frundsberg* units fared a little better, succeeding in breaking through after a second attempt. The remnants of the division re-formed to the north-west of Dresden. *Generalmajor* (*Brigadeführer*) Heinz Harmel was later relieved of his command of *Frundsberg* for his refusal to carry out orders. His punishment was mild considering that at this stage of the war officers and men were being executed for lesser 'crimes'.

On the morning of 21 April, an artillery barrage, preceded by aerial bombing, paved the way for General Aleksey Semenovich Zhadov's infantry formations to break into Spremberg. The town was cleared by Lieutenant General Nikita Lebedenko's 33rd Guards Rifle Corps following fierce close-quarter fighting in which dismounted German tank crews fought as infantry. With his left flank secure, Konev could now concentrate on reducing the German 'Cottbus Group' of forces, which posed a threat to his right flank. He described the bitter fighting around Cottbus as follows:

> On the night of 20–21 April, the tank grouping of the Front arrived at the Berlin outer defensive ring, being approximately thirty-five kilometers distant from the infantry armies on this day. At that time, on our right flank, Gordov's 3rd Army, continuing to fight the most stubborn battles with the Cottbus grouping, not only repulsed strong German counterattacks, but also succeeded in getting on the route to bypass them to the west, having forced them toward the swampy floodplain of the Spree.

In truth, Konev was less than pleased with Gordov's slow progress. Cottbus was directly attacked on 21 April and fell the following day following a fierce battle in which more than 1,000 German defenders were killed and a further eighty-seven committed suicide, including the Fortress Commandant Lieutenant General Ralf Sodan.

11

Tour D: Spremberg–Trebendorf–Kahren–Cottbus

Viewpoint (D1): Spremberg: German Mass Grave

Directions: From your Berlin base, take the A113 in the direction of Schönfeld. Join the A13 and then A14 to Cottbus. At Cottbus-Sud, take the fifth exit onto the B97. Follow Berliner Strasse until you see the Shell garage, then turn right onto Drebkauer Strasse. The entrance to the site (Spremberg Forest Cemetery) is next to a florist's. For satnav users, enter Drebkauer Strasse, 6, Spremberg, Germany.

The Forest Cemetery contains a German mass grave holding the remains of 128 officers and men, sixty-eight of whom are unknown.

Viewpoint (D2): Spremberg: German Cemetery

Directions: Head back down towards Berliner Strasse and then turn left onto Westbahnstrasse. Continue onto Mittlestrasse and Burgstrasse, then take a left onto Pfortenstrasse. Follow the road and then take a left onto Georgenstrasse. Follow the road until you see Weskower Allee on your left, then take the next right onto Kirschallee. Follow the road almost to the bottom, the cemetery comes up on your right just two streets before Goetheplatz. For satnav users, enter Kirschallee, 1, Spremberg, Germany.

The German Cemetery contains the graves of 286 officers and men. In 2011, construction of the OPAL natural gas pipeline was nearing completion in the Halbe area south of Berlin. It was agreed that Spremberg would be one of three designated burial sites, if the remains of military casualties were discovered (the other sites were Halbe and Lietzen).

Viewpoint (D3): Trebendorf: Soviet Memorial and Cemetery

Directions: Head north on Lutherstrasse, then turn right onto Forster Landstrasse. Turn right onto Tuchmacherallee, follow the road until you reach the end and then turn left to join the B156. Follow the road and then and as you pass An den Gärten on the left take the next right onto the L87. Continue down the L87 and Spremberger Strasse. Turn right at the end of Spremberger Strasse and head in the direction of the train halt on Bahnhofstrasse. Continue along Bahnhofstrasse and Schleifer Strasse, which then merges into Dorfstrasse. Follow the road through the wooded area and keep a look out for the cemetery, which then comes up on your right. For satnav users, enter Dorfstrasse, 4, Trebendorf, Germany.

The inauguration of the Soviet cemetery, which contains 535 graves, took place on 29 September 1945. The local inhabitants who remained were forced to attend the ceremony.

Viewpoint (D4): Kahren: German War Graves and Soviet Collective Grave

Directions: Head back up Bahnhofstrasse and Friedenstrasse, then take Gross Dubener Weg and Schleifer Weg in the direction of Groß Düben. Take the L49—Spremberger Strasse to Debern and then turn left onto Forster Strasse. Follow the road, which then becomes the L482 onto Cottbuser Strasse. Continue along the road, which is now the L48. At the end of the L48, turn left onto the L49. Follow the road and then turn left onto the L50 (opposite Kahrener Strasse). Continue along the road, which becomes Kahrener Hauptstrasse, then turn right on Kirschstrasse/Kahrener Hauptstrasse. Turn left onto Frauendorfer Weg, then follow the road until the cemetery comes up on your right. For satnav users, enter Frauendorfer Weg, 13, Kahren (Cottbus), Germany.

The cemetery holds a Soviet collective grave containing the remains of four officers and men. The adjacent German cemetery contains a plot with the grave markers of ninety officers and men.

Viewpoint (D5): Cottbus: Soviet Memorial and Cemetery, and German War Graves

Directions: Head back up Frauendorfer Weg and then join Kahrener Hauptstrasse, which leads on to Karlshofer Strasse. Continue along the road, which then leads on to Bahnhofstrasse and Kiekebuscher Weg. Turn right onto Madlower Hauptstrasse (B168). Continue onto Dresdener Strasse and as you pass Ringstrasse the Cemetery comes up on your right. For satnav users, enter Dresdener Strasse, 35, Cottbus, Germany.

The Soviet Memorial is located within the grounds of the Südfriedhof. The large cemetery grounds contain a plot holding the remains of 742 Soviet officers and men. If you head north-east from Soviet plot, you will find a seperate plot holding the remains of German troops and civilians killed during the Allied air raid of 15 February 1945. If you have time to spare, it is also worth visiting the mass grave of Polish forced labourers, which is located to the north-west of the Soviet plot.

No doubt you be ready for a spot of lunch by now. The centre of Cottbus is certainly worth exploring; local highlights include the art nouveau facade of the State Theatre and the remains of the city fortifications (Spremberg, Munz and Mauer towers). Numerous eateries can be found between Schlosskirchplatz and Berliner Strasse.

Viewpoint (D6): Cottbus: Military Aviation Museum

Directions: From Schlosskirchplatz (Cottbus) head east onto Burgstrasse, then turn right, right again and then left onto Freiheitstrasse. Follow the road and then turn right onto Franz Mehring Strasse, continue along Karl Liebknecht Strasse. Turn right onto Pappelallee. At the roundabout, take the last exit onto Dahlitzer Strasse. Follow the road until you see the museum on your right (directly opposite Strobitzer Haupstrasse). For satnav users, enter Fichtestrasse, 1, Cottbus, Germany.

This fine museum has a varied collection of Second World War and Cold War-era aircraft including a German Fw 190F, Soviet MiG-21 and -23 fighters, and an American F-84F Thunderstreak. Opening hours are Tuesday–Friday (10 a.m.–4 p.m.) and Saturday–Sunday (10 a.m.–5 p.m.).

From November to February, there is limited opening from Tuesday-Saturday (10 a.m.—4 p.m.). The website is flugplatzmuseumcottbus.de; contact: info@flugplatzmuseumcottbus.de. After visiting the museum, you can head back to your Berlin base via the L49, A113, and B96.

History

Spremberg was first mentioned in a document entitled *Opppidium et castrum Sprewenberch,* dating from 1301. The document records the sale of the castle and surrounding areas by the Thuringian Margrave Dietrich IV to Archbishop

Burchard II of Blankenburg. Spremburg passed through numerous hands over the next 150 years, including the aristocratic Schwarzenburg and Kittlitz families. Two major fires in 1556 and 1604 caused extensive damage. Spremberg's woes were by no means over as the plague hit in 1626. Having barely recovered from this calamity, Swedish troops plundered the area six years later during the Thirty Years War. In 1646, another great fire destroyed the town hall and 185 dwellings. A fourth great fire raged through the city five years later, destroying 200 dwellings. Plague struck again in 1680, accounting for approximately half of the local population. Spremburg recovered gradually, but was hit by the fifth and last great fire in 1705, which destroyed almost the whole of the residential district.

Spremberg came under the administration of the Prussian province of Brandenburg following the Treaty of Vienna, which finally drew a line under the Napoleonic era. In 1893, the city celebrated the 1,000th anniversary of its founding. The celebrations were based on the work carried out in 1613 by historian Abraham Hossmann who cited the Burgundian Chronicle as having proved that Spremburg was founded by Emperor Arnulf in the year 893. The chronicle never in fact existed and Hossmann was exposed as a swindler. The celebrations went ahead nonetheless. In 1897, the city was directly connected with Berlin following the completion of the rail link on the Berlin–Görlitz route. This rail link was important as Spremberg was geographically at the very center of the German Reich in the years between 1871 and 1920.

The city was very much a backwater during the war due to an absence of major industries. It was not until early 1945 that the war came home to Spremberg as refugees began to pour into the city. The still functioning rail links also made Spremberg an ideal transport hub for the movement of Allied prisoners who were being evacuated from camps in the line of march of the advancing Red Army. One of the camps evacuated was Stalag Luft III, renowned for *The Wooden Horse* and *The Great Escape*. British prisoners were forced to undertake the gruelling 'Long March' that set off on 27 January 1945 in sub-zero temperatures. The route of the march was retraced in January 2010 in order to commemorate the sixty-fifth anniversary in conditions very similar to those experienced at the time. Amongst those taking part were six veterans, the oldest of whom was Eric Foinette who led the marchers off after celebrating his ninety-fifth birthday. Other marchers included Andy Wiseman:

> It brings back memories of cold and hunger. It is now roughly the same temperature as we had in 1945. I remember the camaraderie and the *esprit de corps*. But it was a good lesson. You learn that cometh the hour, cometh the man. You learn that nothing is impossible. We weren't trained to go on the long march, we were traned to fly. But if you come to a barrier there's no way out but to get over it. It's no good turning round and pretending it's not there.

The author standing by a Soviet anti-tank gun.

The author standing next to a Soviet IS II Stalin tank.

Soviet IS II tanks on the Oder-Neisse front.

Trudging along in deep snow, the prisoners battled on against the elements for thirty-six hours. There was no provision made for food and so the prisoners carried their own cooking pots and what little food they had with them. Accommodation *en route* consisted of an overnight stay in a drafty barn. Few of the prisoners knew at the time if they were being evacuated or being taken to a place of execution.

American prisoners were also evacuated from their separate compound at Stalag Luft III and undertook an equally gruelling forced march to Spremberg via Muskau. One of the marchers was William Miller, who later recalled the suffering endured by those who took part:

> Prisoners were falling to the ground, unable to continue. Our German guards were older men and just could not keep up. I actually saw American officers carrying the German guard's rifles as well as supporting them along the line of march ... It seemed as if we had been on the road for a week. Everyone seemed to be in a daze. Friends whom you had made in the camp didn't recognise you and wouldn't even talk to you. It was every man for himself, and later our senior officers admitted they had lost all control over the situation. At this point, no one could help anyone. You were on your own.

After stumbling into Muskau, the prisoners were quartered for the night in an old tile factory. After completing the second leg of the march to Spremberg, the prisoners were then transferred into cattle cars for the rail journey to Moosburg. The three-day journey was not without incident as the senioir American officer Colonel Charles Goodrich authorised escape attempts by thirty-two men, all were recaptured within one-and-a-half days. The prisoners finally arrived at the vermin infested and overcrowded Stalag VIIA. Here they would remain until the camp was liberated on 29 April by the 14th Armoured Division of General George Patton's 3rd Army.

After the war, Spremberg was rebuilt as approximately two-thirds of the built-up area had been destroyed in the fighting. Between 1950 and 1952, local government reforms overturned the existing administrative boundary areas, effectively increasing the size of the Spremberg district. In October 1989, peaceful pro-democracy demonstrations were held. The end of Communist rule followed with the fall of the Berlin Wall a month later. In May 1990, the first free local elections were held, marking the transition from authoritarianism to democracy.

Cottbus dates back to the establishment of a Wendish settlement in the tenth century. The first official record of the city was in 1156 when it came under the administration of the Margrave of Lusatia. German settlers began to move into the area during the thirteenth century and co-existed peacefully with the Wendish population. The area prospered and Cottbus played a leading role in the expanding wool trade. In 1445, the city was acquired by the Hohenzollerns of Brandenburg. The city flourished and in 1701 formally came under the administration of the Kingdom of Prussia.

Cottbus was largely spared the miseries of war until early 1945. It was not a major industrial centre by any means. However, it became a target for American bombers following intelligence, which showed that the famed Fw 190 and the high-performace Fw Ta 152 interceptor were being assembled at a factory site close to the aerodrome. The major daylight bombing raid carried out in February 1945 was later recounted by teenager Jutta Obst whose father Max worked as a supervisor at Cottbus railway station:

> The power of the explosions broke loose all the doors, including their frames. The wall plaster had fallen off, and the wall hangings and pictures were all broken up; all over the floors. It was a bad scene, a terrible and depressing scene. But we were grateful that we were alive and physically unharmed ...When the attack was over, the house still stood but was substantially damaged.

Those last months of the war brought terror to the population of Cottbus as the fear of air raids was ever present. Gisela Vogt was only seven years old in 1945, but vividly recalled her own experience of being under the aerial barrage of bombs:

> We went to bed with our clothes on so as to be ready for the alarm. Once, we were trapped in the basement, and it took about an hour to dig our way out. I once saw a little black body underneath a burned-out automobile. It apparently was the driver who had tried to hide there. You don't forget those sights and smells.

If the terror of the bombings was not enough, the women and children in the city were advised to leave in March as the Red Army was poised to strike across the Oder. As non-combatants prepared to leave, teenage boys and old men were called to the colours to defend their city.

Cottbus was already swollen with refugees from the eastern provinces, now they too joined the exodus towards Berlin. The column of refugees was overtaken by the advancing Red Army near the village of Stradow. Some refugees, including Jutta Obst's family decided to head back to Cottbus. Jutta recalled the scene:

> Everything around us was burning and on fire. Along the way we passed corpses of dead soldiers and dead horses everywhere. The stench of death filled the air. This gruesome sight of death, heaps of twisted steel and concrete, naked blasted walls, was so enormously frightening ... I remember being so anxious, nervous, scared, and trembling. The other side of the highway was crowded with Russians and their tanks, with trucks, cannon, armoured cars, soldiers, etc.

The Obst family left Cottbus in April 1946 and settled in the western zone of occupation near Frankfurt-am-Main.

Following the fall of Cottbus to the Red Army, the aerodrome was immediately put to use. The three runways remained in operation with Soviet forces until 1952. Four years later, the East German Air Force took over the site. The Air Force Staff was quartered there until a merger with the Air Defence Command at Strausberg led to a relocation of the command staff the following year. Nonetheless, Cottbus remained an important cog in the machine as it was chosen as the home base for the first Air Force combat unit JG 1 *Fritz Schmenkel*. This unit operated MiG-15 and MiG-17 jet fighters until 1958 when the upgraded MiG-17PF was brought into service. In 1967, the squadron received MiG-21 fighter-interceptors. Cottbus's association with JG 1 came to an end in 1982 when the squadron was transferred to Holzdorf.

It is worth noting that the first (and only) female combat pilot in service with the East German forces was based at Cottbus. Iris Witting was a remarkable woman who volunteered for service in the People's Police in 1952. She completed her flight training in 1953, flying with a Soviet instructor in the MiG-15. In early 1954, she graduated and became a fully-fledged pilot in

JG 1. Shortly afterwards she was involved in an accident while piloting a Yak-18 trainer aircraft. Her injuries prevented her from undertaking flying duties again until 1956 when she was involved in engine testing for the Society of Sports and Technology. A year later, she joined Aviator Training Squadron 15 as a flight instructor. Her adventures were recounted in the *Fliegerrevue* journal in an article entitled 'Ramming through Neuhausen'. Witting died in 1978, aged fifty.

Cottbus has experienced something of a renaissance since the reunification of Germany. The city is now home to over 8,000 students attending the Brandenburg University of Technology. Extensive renovation of the city centre has succeeded in restoring some of its old baroque charm. If you can make time during your tour, I would certainly recommend stopping for an extended lunch break in this vibrant and interesting city.

12

Last Laurels

Two days of hard fighting on the vital Seelow Heights sector had seriously weakened the German defenders. The stubborn German defence was still holding in places, but now Zhukov looked towards making the decisive breakthrough, which would take his forces to Berlin. However, before the breakthrough could be achieved, German combat groupings barring the eastern approaches to Berlin had to be destroyed. Chuikov later recalled:

> On 18 April the troops of the 8th Guards Army were given the task, not of taking large stretches of territory, but of giving as much punishment as possible to the enemy's manpower and equipment, both on the field of battle and further back in his defence system ... That day the Nazi command threw into battle two fresh mechanised divisions—the Kurmark and the Müncheberg divisions—and an SS infantry division under the command of General Seizert. Fierce fighting developed. Counterattacks followed one after another, particularly on the Army's left flank. In the Diedersdorf area the Nazis tried to cut the main road Kustrin–Berlin, along which the main mass of our tanks and equipment was moving. This threat had to be averted at all costs.

Chuikov was right to be concerned as his subsequent push towards Müncheberg met with strong resistance. On both the northern flank, Soviet armour suffered heavy losses around Batzlow. To the south, German resistance around Lietzen and Marxdorf served to reduce the rate of the Soviet advance to a crawl. By the evening of 18 April, Chuikov's troops were dug in on the Trebnitz–Jahnsfelde line.

The following morning, Soviet armour attacked from Trebnitz towards Jahnsfelde and Müncheberg. At Jahnsfelde, the 3rd Flak Battalion of the 18th Artillery Regiment was supposedly withdrawing southwards when they were bounced by Soviet tanks. According to some accounts, the German artillery rapidly redeployed in a dip on the crest of a hill near to the crossroads (in my own view, it is more likely that the German guns were already deployed in this position to defend the crossroads). Here, under the command of Captain Muller, the Battalion's 88-mm guns engaged the attacking T-34 tanks. In the fierce battle that followed, the German gunners smashed tank after tank, albeit with heavy loss among their own numbers. This brave action succeeded in temporarily blunting the Soviet advance. I have some doubts concerning the large numbers of T-34s said to have been destroyed (approximately 100). By late afternoon, additional Soviet forces deployed in the area, ready for the next push. Tank forces, supported by artillery and aircraft smashed their way through Jahnsfelde. By 6 p.m., Soviet troops were engaged in heavy fighting against determined German defenders in the northern sector of Müncheberg.

That same day, heavy fighting took place on the approaches to Strausberg. To the north east of the town, Nordland SS *Panzergrenadiers* were engaged in heavy fighting around Protzel and Buckow. Following orders from General Weidling, the reconnaissance battalion of the Nordland Division and a Hitler Youth detachment launched a counter-attack in the Buckow Forest in order to relieve Soviet pressure. The attack was a complete failure and both units were badly mauled. The survivors made their way to Strausberg, which was already under imminent threat of encirclement by Katukov's 1st Guards Tank Army. King Tiger Tanks of the 503rd Heavy Panzer Battalion were on hand to stem the advance of Katukov's armoured spearheads along the road leading from Bollendorf to Strausberg. In a classic tank action, the 503rd savaged the Soviet armour, which was caught in the act of refuelling. In this one action, 105 Soviet tanks were destroyed and a further seventy-six damaged. Throughout the campaign, Soviet losses in men and materiel were disproportionate. However, no matter how many casualties the German defenders inflicted on their enemy, they simply could not hold their extended front indefinitely.

Unrelenting Soviet pressure began to tell. By the evening of 19 April, Bezarin's 5th Shock Army had reached the outskirts of Strausberg. The following day, fighting centred around the airfield that had been recently evacuated by Luftwaffe personnel. The fighting for Strausberg was brief but bloody. The tenacious defence put up by the Danmark and Norge Regiments inflicted more casualties on the Soviet forces. However, they could not hold and so withdrew in a south-westerly direction towards Berlin. The following day, Soviet troops from the 32nd Corps of the 5th Shock Army successfully secured Strausberg.

The German defence performed brilliantly in these last battles on the approaches to Berlin. Even at this terminal stage of the war, the battered remnants of once proud divisions, along with newly raised units managed to inflict stunning tactical defeats on an enemy who outnumbered them 10:1. Yet, for all their bravery and skill, the German forces were simply not strong enough to stop the advance of a military colossus inured to massive casualties.

13

Tour E: Jahnsfelde–Buckow–Strausberg–Altlandsberg–Ahrensfelde

Viewpoint (E1): Jahnsfelde: Crossroads

Directions: From your Berlin base, take the B1 towards Muncheburg. Continue along the B1 until you reach Jahnsfelde. There is a parking area at the Landgasthaus Jahnsfelde (opens at 11 a.m.). From the parking area you get a good view of the woods in front of which the three German gun batteries supposedly rapidly deployed to take on the Soviet armour. Alternatively, turn right at the crossroads and follow the L36 until you come to the first turn-off on your right. This road will bring you out just behind the German gun positions. For satnav users, enter Schmiedestrasse, 1, Jahnsfelde (Müncheberg), Germany. Or, if you wish to park closer to the German positions, enter Trebnitzer Strasse, 1, Jahnsfelde (Müncheberg), Germany (the L36 is opposite Trebnitzer Strasse, therefore turn right instead of left when you approach the destination.

The stand made by the 3rd (Flak) Battalion of the 18th Artillery Regiment at Jahnsfelde halted the Soviet advance on Muncheburg for several hours. The losses incurred by the battalion were considerable; the unit effectively ceased to exist.

Viewpoint (E2): Buckow: Memorial and Soviet Cemetery

Directions: Head west on the B1/Seelower Strasse in the direction of Müncheberg. At the roundabout, continue straight onto Ernst-Thalmann Strasse/B168. Continue along the B168/Eberswalder Chaussee to Waldsieversdorf. Turn right onto the K6413/Berliner Strasse. Turn right onto Neue Promenade. At the end of the road, turn right onto Lindenstrasse.

Continue along the road, passing the Markische Schweiz Arboretum on your left, the memorial and cemetery then comes up on your right. For satnav users, enter, Lindenstrasse, 14, Buckow (Markische Schweiz), Germany.

This interesting memorial is designed in the shape of an aircraft wing framed by a propeller. Three plaques are inscribed with the names of seventy officers and men of the Soviet Air Force. The plaque on the right of the memorial carries a simple inscription in German, which can be translated as, 'Honour their Memory'.

If you wish to explore some of the stunning scenery around Buckow, the *Markische Schweiz* Nature Park is well worth a visit. The hiking trail takes you past some picturesque lakes and valleys. Guided walks can be arranged at the *Schweizerhaus* Visitor Center (Lindenstrasse, 33, Buckow). From a historical perspective, the walks are certainly worth doing as they take you close to some of the areas where the failed German counter-attack in the Buckow Woods took place.

Viewpoint (E3) Strausberg: German War Graves

Directions: From the memorial, head back down Lindenstrasse, then turn right onto Weinbergsweg. Turn right onto Wriezener Strasse/K6413. Turn left onto Reichenberger Chaussee, then continue along Hauptstrasse/E34. Continue along the L34/Alt-Ruhlsdorf. Continue along Dorfstrasse/Hohensteiner Chaussee until you are in the town centre, then turn left onto An der Stadtmauer. Turn left onto August-Bebel Strasse/Berliner Strasse. Continue along Berliner Strasse until you see the Evangelic Church coming up on your right. For satnav users, enter Berliner Strasse, 103, Strausberg, Germany.

The Evangelic Cemetery St Marien contains a plot holding the remains of German troops who fell in the battles along the approaches to Berlin.

History

Strausberg was founded in 1240. However, it was another ninety-three years before the town's first town hall was built. Strausberg flourished, particularly following the industrialisation of the nineteenth century. A growing class consciousness among the workers led to the founding of trade unions. Later, branches of the Social Democratic Party and the Communist Party of Germany were established in the town. The democratic leanings of many prominent trade unionists and politicians brought them into conflict with the

The author at Jahnsfelde. (*Author's collection*)

Soviet howitzer.

National Socialists following their rise to power in 1933. Many were seen as enemies of the state and were subsequently arrested and taken into 'protective custody' in the so-called 'Wild Camps' set up by the Stormtroopers.

In February 1945, a series of tank-traps were constructed to defend the town against attack by the Red Army. That same month also saw the transfer from the town of the aircraft repair facility and the Luftwaffe Navigation School. Strausberg experienced a heavy Soviet air raid on 16 April, which the residents later referred to as 'Black Monday.' The mill, freight yards and schools were all hit and casualties were heavy. Only some 200–300 residents stayed behind following the withdrawal of German forces four days later. On the evening of 20 April, Georg Kurtze, a seventy-two-year-old Social Democrat, and former inmate of the concentration camp at Oranienburg, hoisted a white flag from the town hall in a bid to save Strausberg from further destruction. Kurtze's lifeless body was found on Badstrasse several days later. He had been shot in the head at close range. Nonetheless, his gesture had proved successful as the town was occupied without further incident on 21 April. The occupying authorities later renamed Ritterstrasse (the Kurtze family lived at No. 11), Georg-Kurtze Strasse. In April 2005, the mayor Peter Thierfeld attended a ceremony at Kurtze's graveside to celebrate his life as an anti-Nazi and to commemorate the 'liberation' of Strausberg.

This would be a good time to stop off for a spot of lunch. There are numerous cafes, fast-food outlets and restaurants within a short walk of St

Buckow Soviet memorial. (*Lienhard Schulz, Wikimedia Commons*)

Marien Cemetery. It may also be worth extending your visit to this charming town by taking a look at the *Heimatmuseum,* which is located between the cemetery and the town centre (August-Bebel Strasse, 33, Strausberg). The museum has a permanent exhibition chronicling life in Strausberg from the earliest settlers to the present day.

Viewpoint (E4): Altlandsberg: Soviet Mass Grave

Directions: From the cemetery on Berliner Strasse, head in a southerly direction (away from the town centre). Take a right turn onto Altlandsberger Chaussee. Turning left, continue to follow the Chaussee/ L33. Turn right onto Wolshagen and then continue along Strausberger Strasse. At the end of Strausberger Strasse you will come to Am Markt where there is ample parking. The mass grave is sited on the far corner of the square.

History

Altlandsberg was founded on the site of a former settlement of the Slavic Spevani tribe who lived around the River Spree. The area was resettled following the period of *Ostsiedlung* (German eastward expansion) initiated by the Holy Roman Emperor Charlemagne. In 928–929, Henry I (Henry the Fowler) conquered Brandenburg and imposed tribute on the Slavic tribes. Albert the Bear later assimilated the Slavic peoples into the German settler population. In 1335, Margrave Louis I established a Sevite (servants of Mary) monastery, which was later dissolved during the Protestant Reformation. The town was devastated during the Hussite Wars (1419–1434) and in the following century was ravaged by the plague. In 1632, the town was burnt to the ground during the Thirty Years War.

Altlandsberg was largely spared from the ravages of war as colonel general Bezarin's troops quickly pushed on towards Berlin in order to assist in sealing off the city. In May 1945, the Ulbricht group of the German Communist Party flew from Moscow to Miedzyrzec (Meseritz), from where they were driven to their new headquarters in Bruchmuhle (incorporated into Altlandsberg in 2002). In June 1945, Ulbricht and the other group leaders (Ackermann and Sobottka) travelled back to Moscow to meet with Stalin and Andrei Zhdanov. Stalin's instructions were to create a 'Party of the People.' The party leaders then set about developing policies geared to the establishment of an anti-fascist democratic republic.

On 11 June 1945, the Communist Party of Germany was officially relaunched and subsequently managed to win some seats in the *Bundestag* (West German Parliament) elections in 1949. Thereafter, the fortunes of the party declined. In 1956, the party was banned in West Germany. A small fringe party emerged in 1969, but lacking popular support made little headway in the political arena. In East Germany, the party was merged with the Social Democratic Party in 1989. The reformed party struggled to distance itself from its Marxist-Leninist past and in 1990 was rebranded as the Party of Democratic Socialism. In 2007, the party merged with the western-based Labour and Social Justice—The Electoral Alternative party to form *Der Linke* (The Left), which found greater acceptance in the former West German state. By 2013, *Der Linke* was the fourth largest political party in Germany.

Viewpoint (E5): Altlandsberg: German War Graves

Directions: From Am Markt, turn left onto Berliner Strasse. Continue along Berliner Strasse/Berliner Allee. The cemetery containing the war graves comes up on your left just before An der Promenade. For satnav users, enter Berliner Allee, 8, Altlandsberg, Germany.

The cemetery contains an ornate grave from the First World War, and a mass grave holding the remains of those killed during the latter days of the Second World War.

Viewpoint (E6): Ahrensfelde: Soviet Memorial and Cemetery

Directions: Head away from the town centre down Berliner Allee/Honower Chaussee. Turn right onto An der Muhle, following the road until you reach the end. Turn left onto Altlandsberger Weg. Continue along Altlandsberger Weg/Mehrower Dorfstrasse/Mehrower Chaussee/Mehrower Strasse. At the bottom of Mehrower Strasse, turn left onto Dorfstrasse, then turn right onto Lindenberger Strasse. Follow the road until you see the memorial and cemetery coming up on your right as you pass Bahnstrasse. For satnav users, enter Lindenberger Strasse, 8, Ahrensfelde, Germany.

The Soviet Cemetery at Ahrensfelde holds the remains of 120 officers and men who fell in combat on the approaches to Berlin.

History

Ahrensfelde was first recorded in the *Landbuch* (Domesday Book) commissioned by the Emperor Charles IV following the Golden Bull of 1356. The nearby Blumberg Manor was acquired by one of Frederick the Great's favourite poets, Friedrich von Canitz, in the late seventeenth century.

The manor was later redesigned by the prominent architect Karl Friedrich Schinkel. In April 1945, the manor was severely damaged by plundering Red Army soldiers.

Ahrensfelde features in the James Patterson and Mark Sullivan crime thriller *Private Berlin*, published in 2013. The story is based around Mattie Engel who works for the detective agency Private Berlin. The body of her colleague and fiancée Chris is found in an old slaughterhouse in Ahrensfelde along with scores of other people who had all been brutally murdered. As Mattie begins her investigations, the slaughterhouse explodes, obliterating all of the evidence. Mattie realises that a serial killer is at loose and that she could be the next victim. However, I assure you that you will be quite safe in Ahrensfelde.

If you have time to spare, the Soviet Mausoleum and Cemetery located in Berlin-Marzahn is only a short drive away (Wiesenburger Weg, 7, Berlin-Marzahn).

14

Retreat

On the night of 19 April, Marshal Rokossovsky reported to Stalin that his Front was ready to go on the offensive. He intended to launch his assault the following morning along a 48-kilometre front, stretching from Altdamm in the north (now in Poland and known as Szczecin) to Schwedt in the south. Colonel General Pavel Batov's 65th Army led the attack, crossing the Oder under a smokescreen. By the end of the day, his units had established a lodgement on the western bank of the river, which extended just under 5 kilometres and was approximately 2 kilometres deep. Attacks by the 49th and 70th Army units did not fare as well as a result of poor reconnaissance and the fact that Batov's bridgehead was vulnerable to counterattack.

During the night of 20–21 April, repeated German counterattacks were beaten off by Batov's troops. Over the next day, he extended the frontage of his bridgehead to just over 8 kilometres and a depth of approximately 3 kilometres. Meanwhile, the 70th Army made some progress in clearing parts of the flooded areas to the north of Schwedt. The fortunes of the hapless 49th Army had hardly improved as German pressure against its narrow bridgehead prevented any meaningful tactical manoeuvring. Rokossovsky did not enjoy the same force to space ratio as Zhukov or Konev. His limited bridgeheads also meant that he would be forced to concentrate his available combat power along the right flank. The task of clearing the Germans from their well organised defences would be tricky and time consuming.

The German defence in General Hasso von Manteuffel's 3rd Panzer Army sector was generally holding firm. Soviet forces only had only succeeded in developing one significant bridgehead to the south of Altdamm, which stretched roughly along the line of Kurow to Siadło Górne (Hohenzahden) and had penetrated towards Schillersdorf. Heinrici later recalled the situation in Manteuffel's sector following German counterattacks on 21 April:

> The enemy was pushed back, but not driven off from the western bank of the Oder. New forces had already been brought over the Oder at night. They strengthened the bridgehead and were now clinging to the steep bank of the Oder that provided cover. From here they initiated a counter-attack and again enlarged the bridgehead to the west. The experience gained in Russia several times proved to be true in this case too: once the Russians had gained ground on the enemy's riverside, it was almost impossible to drive them off from there again. They quickly and skilfully entrenched themselves into the slopes running down towards the river and could neither really be reached by artillery or by mortars. Their way back was blocked by the water and the commissars standing on the other side of the river, who without any qualms shot fleeing soldiers. Thus the Russians were clinging to the earth and holding out, for only holding on could offer them a slight chance to save their lives.

The breach in the German lines described by Heinrici came at a time when the whole situation along the Oder Front was deteriorating. Zhukov and Konev's fronts had gained freedom to manoeuvre and, while not advancing at the same rate, Rokossovsky's front had tied down 3rd Panzer Army, thus depriving it of the opportunity to launch a counterblow in the direction of Berlin. The culmination point in the battle along the Oder Front had been reached.

Soviet propaganda leaflet 1945, 'Capitulate: it's your only chance to be saved'. (*Author's collection*)

Manteuffel knew the Red Army as well as Heinrici. Like Heinrici, he was a realist and knew the Soviet tide could not be held back indefinitely. His plan was to hold on as long as possible and, after having done his duty, retreat 'step by step, with my soldiers arm to arm, shoulder to shoulder, all the way to the west.' His depleted Panzer Army did sterling work holding the line, but was not in a position to further influence the decisive battle for Berlin. Hitler knew this too and now looked for salvation in the form of General Felix Steiner's 'Army Group Steiner'. The plan Hitler concocted was bold and imaginative: Steiner's troops were to strike southwards from Eberswalde and hit Zhukov's flank. At the same time, Busse's 9th Army was to attack northwards and link up with Steiner's forces. The attack plan issued to Steiner was as follows:

> It is the exclusive task of Army Group Steiner to attack with the 4th SS Police Division and, if possible, with strong forces of the 5th Jaeger Division and the 25th *Panzergrenadier* Division, which is to be released by the 3rd Marine Division. Attacking forces are to link with units of the 56th Panzer Corps (SS Division Nordland), 18th *Panzergrenadier* Division, 20th *Panzergrenadier* Division, Panzer Division Müncheberg, and parts of the 9th Parachute Division. This link is to be defended at all costs. It is expressly forbidden to fall back to the west. Officers who do not comply unconditionally with this order are to be arrested and to be immediately shot. You [Steiner] are liable with your head for the execution of this order. The fate of the German Reich's capital depends on the success of your mission.

The plan may have been bold and imaginative, but Steiner had no intention of carrying it out as his available forces were no more than a weak miscellany of units based around the depleted III (Germanic) SS Panzer Corps; Army Group Steiner was an army in name only.

Despite being answerable with his head, Steiner declined to launch the attack that Hitler had ordered. At first, Heinrici agreed, stating to General Krebs that, 'Steiner does not have the strength to make such an attack.' However, Heinrici's growing concern regarding the threat of a Soviet wedge being driven between the 3rd Panzer Army and the 9th Army led him to issue an urgent order to Steiner:

> The attack into the deep flank of the enemy, who is thrusting to the west, has to be carried out this evening (22 April) without waiting for the still missing units of the assault troops. First objective is Wensickendorf-Wandlitz-Autobahn and east thereof. I expect that you will exert all your energies and strength for the success of this decisive attack. You have to report to me on the starting of the operation.

During the afternoon conference, General Jodl announced the disconcerting news that Soviet forces were tightening the noose around Berlin. Hitler demanded to know what progress Steiner's forces were making. After a long and uncomfortable silence, General Krebs told Hitler that no attack had taken place as Steiner was not able to mobilise the necessary forces. A key witness to Hitler's reaction was Gerhard Bolt (cavalry officer seconded to the military intelligence section Foreign Armies East). In his book *Hitler's Last Days: An Eye-Witness Account*, Boldt described the angry scenes that followed Krebs' revelation:

> Hitler was told that the attack had never been launched, and that the withdrawal from Berlin of several units of Steiner's army, on Hitler's orders, had so weakened the front that the Russians had broken through to Berlin. That was too much for Hitler. He asked everyone except Wilhelm Keitel, Alfred Jodl, Hans Krebs, and Wilhelm Burgdorf to leave the room. Then Hitler started jumping up and down, while he ranted and raved. His face turned purple in turns, and he was shaking all over. His voice kept breaking, as he screamed out the words disloyalty, cowardice, treachery and

Soviet propaganda from 1945: 'Hitler's Germany'. (*Author's collection*)

> insubordination. There followed accusations against the Wehrmacht and the Waffen-SS, of the kind that previous explosions had brought out in a somewhat milder form. His outburst culminated in the oath that he would remain in Berlin ... that he would lead the fight personally.

This was the same Hitler who had declared he would commit suicide following the disastrous failure of his attempt to seize power by force in 1923. Now, faced with the catastrophic disenchantment brought about by Steiner's failure to attack, he once again talked of not being able to go on. It was left to General Jodl to point out to Hitler that if he took his own life, the nation would be leaderless. He also pointed out that the game was not over by stating that Schorner's forces and General Walter Wenck's 12th Army could be brought into play.

Hitler now saw Wenck as Berlin's saviour. If his forces could disengage from the Americans on the Elbe and then head east to link up with Busse's 9th Army, Berlin could yet be relieved. Furthermore, if Steiner's forces and Manteuffel's 3rd Panzer Army could strike towards Berlin from the north, the Soviet forces could be dealt a mighty blow that, even at this late hour, could turn certain defeat into victory—such was his fantasy.

General Keitel arrived at Wenck's headquarters in the Weisenburg forest in the early hours of 23 April. Wenck listened patiently to the fantastical plan that had emerged from the heated military conference several hours earlier. The bombastic Field Marshal paced the room and said in an agitated tone:

> Hitler has broken down completely. Worse, he has given up. Because of this situation, you must turn your troops around and drive towards Berlin, together with the Ninth Army of Busse. The Battle of Berlin has begun. No less than the fate of Germany and Hitler are at stake. It is your duty to attack and save the *Führer*.

Wenck replied automatically, 'of course, Field Marshal, we will do what you order.' At the same time Wenck was weighing up in his mind what could actually be achieved with the limited forces available to him. Without tanks and artillery, his forces did not have a hope of breaking into Berlin. However, he considered his young and eager divisions just strong enough to mount a drive towards Jüterbog and achieve a link-up with Busse's beleaguered 9th Army. Wenck had no intention of sacrificing his men needlessly on the Reich's funeral pyre. However, a general move in the direction of Berlin made sense if he could create a corridor that would allow Busse's forces to break out to the west.

Keitel left Wenck's headquarters at approximately 3 a.m., with the promise that an attack to relieve Berlin would be launched without delay. Wenck waited until Keitel's car had pulled away before calling his staff together. He then outlined how the operation would actually proceed:

> Now, here's how we can actually do it. We will drive as close to Berlin as we can, but we will not give up our positions on the Elbe. With our flanks on the river we keep open a channel of escape to the west. It would be nonsense to drive towards Berlin only to be encircled by the Russians. We will try for a link-up with the Ninth Army, and then let's get out every soldier and civilian who can make it to the west.

Heinrici at first welcomed the drive towards Berlin by Wenck's Army, then he discovered the truth. In a heated telephone call to General Krebs, he denounced the whole plan as madness:

> It's a phantom army. It simply does not have the strength to drive towards the Ninth, join with it and head north to relieve Berlin. There'll be little left of either army by the time they meet—and you know it!

Heinrici's assessment was absolutely correct in that the 9th Army was already fighting for its very existence, while the 3rd Panzer Army was in imminent danger of being encircled by the converging thrusts of Zhukov and Rokossovsky's Fronts. The only force available to strike a blow against Zhukov's troops was Steiner's weak army. Steiner refused to attack, stating to Heinrici that, 'I have hardly any artillery, very few panzers and only a few anti-aircraft guns. I'll tell you what I have; a completely mixed-up heap that will never reach Spandau from Germendorf.' Knowing that Steiner was unlikely to attack, Heinrici began planning to extricate what forces he could from the jaws of the Soviet vice.

Heinrici had only just returned to his own headquarters when the telephone rang. He took the call himself. On the other end of the line was Manteuffel who said, 'I must have your permission to withdraw from Stettin and Schwedt. I cannot hold any longer. If we don't pull out now we'll be encircled.' Heinrici thought for a moment and then replied, 'Retreat. Did you hear me? I said retreat. And listen, Manteuffel. Give up the Stettin Fortress at the same time.' Heinrici then consulted his staff regarding the policy he was to pursue from this point onwards:

> It no longer depends on nice phrases and feelings, this is a matter of life and death. I can no longer bear the responsibility of carrying out this senseless suicide order. Not one more German soldier is to be needlessly sacrificed. I have this responsibility to my troops, people and to someone else higher than Hitler. We hold on *Wotan* 48 hours to give Steiner a chance to attack. Then

> two days on the *Ucker* Line. If we don't, we'll be retreating west, Steiner will be attacking south and he can be cut off.

What Heinrici was planning was a phased withdrawal to the west, contravening Hitler's express orders that specifically prohibited any large-scale retreats. In order to allay suspicion, Heinrici contrived to cover the withdrawals by falsifying his reports. His operations officer Colonel Hans Georg Eismann recalled in his post-war account:

> Since the operations officer was responsible for these reports, it was my job to edit them accordingly. As much as any inaccurate report during a war is to be detected, this was the only path which could be taken in this case.

The staged withdrawal began, but by 27 April, it had become less orderly as units began to crack under constant Soviet pressure.

It took Keitel fewer than forty-eight hours to realise that Heinrici was acting independently of the High Command. He arranged to meet Heinrici and Manteuffel at a crossroads near Fürstenberg. Manteuffel's Chief of Staff General Burkhart Müller-Hillebrand anticipated trouble and, in a post-war interview, outlined his countermeasures:

> I knew there might be a disastrous end to the conference, by which perhaps Manteuffel and Heinrici might be arrested on the spot, and God know what their fate might be. I called in my aide, and I think it was the headquarters company commander, and the quartermaster. I told them that I thought both Heinrici and Manteuffel were in danger. I ordered them to take machine-pistols [and] if anything happened—and I wasn't sure exactly what would happen—they were to protect Heinrici and Manteuffel from arrest or anything else which might occur... I told them that no matter what happened, Manteuffel and Heinrici were to be protected, even if it meant shooting Keitel.

The meeting took place as arranged on the afternoon of 28 April. Keitel immediately launched into a blistering attack on Heinrici screaming out accusation after accusation. Heinrici, 'Why did you move back? You were ordered to stay on the Oder! Hitler ordered you to hold. He ordered you not to move!' Heinrici listened before calmly responding with, 'I cannot hold the Oder with the troops I have. I need reserves. With the troops I have, we will probably have to retreat even further back.' Manteuffel backed Heinrici up by stating that, 'I regret to tell you, that General Heinrici is right. I will have to withdraw even farther unless I get reinforcements. I'm here to find out whether I get them or not.' There would be no reinforcements—the cupboard was bare. An attempt to force Manteuffel into turning his army around failed, and realising that nothing he could either say or do was going to influence the operational situation, Keitel stormed off, yelling, 'You will have to take the responsibility of this action before history.' Manteuffel retorted by saying, 'I, Hasso von Manteuffel, gladly accept this responsibility.' Keitel then turned on Heinrici shouting, 'You are the one! You!' He then relieved Heinrici of command and ordered him to return to his headquarters to hand over to his successor.

After Keitel had driven away, Müller-Hillebrand and his men emerged from the woods. Each was holding a machine-pistol. There had been no serious trouble, but Manteuffel expressed concern for Heinrici's safety, even offering to form a bodyguard to protect him. Heinrici declined and returned to his headquarters as ordered. That evening, the High Command received further reports of forces moving contrary to orders. These reports strengthened the resolve of Keitel and Jodl to dispense with Heinrici's services. The following day, Keitel telephoned Heinrici to confirm his dismissal. It did not matter any longer; the life of Army Group Vistula was coming to an end. Roads were clogged with troops and civilians heading in one direction, away from the dreaded Red Army to safety in the west. The High Command in vain attempted to stem the flood and establish a solid line of defence. The pace of Soviet advances made this impossible. Signs of disintegration were everywhere. Berlin would not be relieved and the forces allocated for Hitler's suicidal rescue operation now sought to extricate themselves from the unfolding chaos by making their way to the west.

The retreat ordered by Heinrici was done just in the nick of time. On 23 April, Rokossovsy was directed to abandon any attempt to encircle Berlin from the north and instead drive westwards towards Stettin. Finally breaking out of their bridgeheads, Batov's tanks advanced to the north-west to isolate German groupings located to the north-east of the Stettin–Neubrandenburg–Rostock line. The advance of Rokossovsky's troops was irresistible and Manteuffel was compelled to abandon his headquarters at Neubrandenburg. On 28 April, the nearby Stalag II-A was liberated, prompting jubilant scenes by American, French, Italian, and Serb prisoners. For the 3,000 surviving Soviet prisoners, the coming of the Red Army was a bittersweet experience. Those suspected of collaboration were shot, while the remainder were given weapons and a chance to atone for their sins by shedding their blood for the motherland.

The liberated Allied prisoners watched as Soviet rocket launchers lay waste to Neubrandenburg. Soviet troops were already on the outskirts where they conducted an unrestrained orgy of rape and violence. In the woods between Stalag II-A and the town, the bodies of several German girls and women hung from the trees, each had been raped and their throats slit. Following his liberation, Father Francis Sampson stayed in the camp in order to assist with the difficult duty of liaising with the Soviet authorities. He soon became aware of atrocities from the reports of other liberated prisoners who had been into the town to look for food. He went out to investigate and discovered the local priest sitting in his burnt-out rectory. Nearby, his mother and two sisters sat huddled on a couch. All three had been raped. Such terrible acts, which for so long had carried out on foreign soil, were now being visited on the German population. As usual, it was defenceless civilians who suffered the most.

In Demmin, Rokossovsky's troops carried out similar acts of brutality after which the old town was burnt to the ground. These acts were partly a result of the desire for revenge. However, a major contributing factor was the powerful hate campaign carried out by Soviet writers and propagandists Ilya Ehrenburg, Konstantin Simonov, and Aleksey Surkov. Their words were translated into practice by the rank and file who for the most part little understood their true darker meaning. When Rokossovsky's troops crossed onto German soil, the 'Order of the Day' read:

> The time has come for a total reckoning with the Fascists, for all their cruelty and atrocities, for the grief and torment of our people, for the blood and tears of our fathers and mothers, wives and children, for the Soviet towns and villages destroyed and plundered by the enemy.

Marshal Rokossovsky.

As they advanced deeper into Germany, Soviet troops were exhorted to carry out acts of brutality, fuelled by intoxicating articles published in *Pravda* and front-line newspapers. Ilya Ehrenburg wrote:

> We advance into Germany, and behind us lie Stalingrad, the Ukraine and Belorussia. We advance through the ashes of our towns and villages, over the traces of blood of Soviet citizens who were tortured and mutilated by the Fascist beast. Woe to the land of murderers! Nothing will stop us now! We have sworn on the graves of our dead friends, we have solemnly promised our children not to rest until the offenders have been dealt with. For the deaths, for the suffering of Our Soviet people, the Fascist robbers shall pay with vast quantities of their own black blood.

Constant repetition of the theme of revenge incited troops to commit dreadful acts. Officers, too, were not immune from the unrelenting pressure. When junior officer Leonid Rabichev was invited by his men to select a girl from

Soviet propaganda: 'Year 1945: as you sow, so shall you reap'.

a group of captives, he felt compelled to go along with them for fear of being branded a coward.

Despite the constant diet of hate propaganda, there were some who were deeply shocked by the atrocities they witnessed. Lev Kopelev was a propaganda officer and interpreter during the Soviet drive across East Prussia. He saw at first hand the senseless burning of towns and villages, which led him to sharply criticise these wanton acts. He was subsequently arrested and charged with 'bourgeois humanitarianism' and 'compassion towards the enemy.' For these crimes, he received a ten year sentence in the Gulag. As it became increasingly clear that the Nazi state was on the verge of collapse, Stalin instituted a change of policy in terms of the propaganda message. Ehrenburg was criticised in *Pravda* on 14 April by Georgy Aleksandrov who penned an article entitled 'Comrade Ehrenburg Oversimplifies.' Six days later, Stalin issued an order of the day laying out how troops should behave in future:

> The armies must change their attitude toward German prisoners and the civilian population, and treat Germans better.
>
> The harsh treatment of Germans is causing them to react with terror and encouraging them to resist stubbornly, refusing to surrender.
>
> The German population, fearing revenge, is organising itself in bands. Such a development is not helpful to us.

Issuing new guidelines was one thing, but implementing them was another as Ehrenburg remained extremely popular with the troops. The hatred for the Germans that had been inculcated in the minds of Soviet troops for so long could now not simply be switched off. What had been the strength of the Red Army now became a weakness as their ability to kill and conquer on a massive scale did little to win the hearts and minds of those people now under Moscow's dominion.

15

Tour F: Eberswalde–Schwedt–Angermünde–Oranienburg

Viewpoint (F1): Eberswalde: Soviet Garrison Cemetery

Directions: From your Berlin base, take the B109 and A114 northwards. At the 1-Dreieck Pankow junction use the right lane to follow signs for the A10 towards Frankfurt/O. Prenzlau/Berliner Ring. As you come up to exit 36—Berlin-Weissensee, join the A11in the direction of Bernau bei Berlin. Follow the A11 until you come to exit 12—Finowfurt, then join the B167 (Eberswalder Strasse). Continue along the B167, which becomes Heegermuhler Strasse until you come up to the Cafe Restaurant Wider Eber. The Cemetery entrance is next to the Restaurant. For satnav users, enter Heegermuhler Strasse, 16, Eberswalde, Germany.

The Soviet Garrison Cemetery was created in 1946 and holds the graves of 860 military personnel and civilians. The cemetery was in use between 1946 and 1967. In 2008, the administration of the cemetery and grounds was taken over by the state of Brandenburg.

Viewpoint (F2): Schwedt: German War Graves and Soviet Cemetery

Directions: Head west on Heegermuhler Strasse, then take a right turn onto Boldstrasse. Follow the road that becomes Britzer Strasse (L237). Join the L23 in the direction of Britz. Continue along the L23 and A11, then take exit 9-Joachimsthal for the B198 towards Angermünde. Join the B2 continuing along the Oder-Neisse-Trasse. Turn right onto the B166/B2 to Zum Beyerswald. Turn left onto Neuer Friedhof, the cemetery then comes up on your right. For satnav users, enter Neuer Friedhof, 2, Schwedt, Germany.

The plot containing sixty-six German war graves and the Soviet Cemetery stand next to each other in the western and north-western sections of the cemetery.

Viewpoint (F3): Angermünde: Soviet Memorial

Directions: Head back along Zum Beyerswald to the B2. Continue along the B2 to Angermünde. As you come into Angemunde, follow Schwedter Strasse/Klosterstrasse and then turn left onto Berliner Strasse. Follow Berliner Strasse until you come to the roundabout, then take the first exit onto Strasse des Friedens. The entrance to the memorial comes up on your left. For satnav users, enter Strasse des Friedens, 4, Angermünde, Germany.

The Soviet memorial is based on a simple design and sits unobtrusively in the Friedens Park (Freedom Park). The inscription on the memorial translates as 'Glory to the Heroes.'

Viewpoint (F4): Oranienburg: Sachsenhausen Concentration Camp Memorial

Directions: Follow Strasse des Friedens and then the B198. As you cross the bridge over the A11, turn right and then follow the road around until it takes you under the bridge and onto the A11. Follow the A11 in the direction of Wandlitz, then turn right onto the B273. Follow the B273 (Bernauer Strasse) and then turn right onto Strasse der Einheit. Turn right onto Strasse der Nationen and then follow the road until you come to the car/coach park on your left. For satnav users, enter Strasse der Nationen, 22, Oranienburg, Germany.

If you wish to stop off for lunch in Oranienburg before visiting the camp memorial site, there are plenty of eateries and food outlets along Bernauer strasse, which runs through the town centre towards Schlossplatz. There are places to eat at the camp memorial site, but they can become a little busy during the summer season.

Sachsenhausen was designed by SS Second Lieutenant Bernhard Kuiper. The site was constructed in the shape of an isosceles triangle, with the apex at the rear of the camp and the two equal sides forming the camp boundary. The base of the camp housed the gate house and administration building from which the whole camp could be observed. The wooden barracks were built on a semicircle around the roll-call square. It was in this square that prisoners of the Penal Commando were forced to test army boots by marching around on a specially marked out test track. Many prisoners lost toes and suffered gangrene due to this work. In 1947, the civilian director of the boot testing operation Ernst Brennscheidt was sentenced to fifteen years in prison by a Soviet tribunal.

The first prisoners incarcerated in the camp were those placed into 'Protective Custody' for real or perceived political offences. By the end of 1936, the camp held 1,600 prisoners. Later, the camp held several other categories of prisoners including Jews, homosexuals, career criminals, asocial elements, Jehovah's Witnesses, Soviet prisoners of war, and Allied commandos or agents. Prominent figures held in Sachsenhausen included Pastor Martin Niemoller, former Austrian chancellor Kurt von Schuschnigg, Goerg Elser (responsible for planting the bomb in the Burgerbraukeller in November 1939), Herschel Grynzpan (carried out the assassination of the German diplomat Ernst von Rath in Paris in November 1938), Yakov Dzhugashvili (Stalin's son), and three escapees from Stalag Luft III (*The Great Escape*): Sydney Dowse, Johnnie Dodge, and Jimmy James.

From the car and coach park, walk past the bistro and toilet block towards the information centre (audio guides are available from the information centre, but are not essential). In front of the information centre, you will see a large metal model of the camp area that you can use to orientate yourself.

Soviet propaganda from 1945: 'Glory to heroes'.

Follow the path leading to the main site, noting the former SS barracks on your right (now used as a police training school). The next building you will see is a single story green painted wooden structure formerly known by prisoners as the 'Green Monster.' The building has been recently renovated (though has still not been opened to visitors at time of writing in October 2015), and housed the dining hall and recreation rooms used by the SS guards (it is often mistaken as the site for the camp brothel, which was located next to the infirmary).

Carry on following the path, noting as you go the photographs depicting the liberation of the camp on the perimeter wall opposite the 'Green Monster.' The entrance to the camp memorial comes up on your left. As you enter, you will note directly ahead the camp administration building with the clock set at 11.07 a.m.—the exact time the camp was liberated on 22 April 1945.

To your right, you will see the main museum building, which dates from the opening of the camp memorial site on 23 April 1961. Over 100,000 people attended the opening ceremony at a time when the Eichmann Trial was ongoing in Jerusalem and the Berlin Wall was not yet built. On entering the museum, you will note a magnificent stained glass window depicting the liberation of the camp. The entrance to the exhibition areas is through the door on your left. There are two main exhibition areas, the first covering the National Socialist period, and the second, the Communist period. To the rear of the museum is a small cafe that sells cold drinks, coffee, sandwiches, and cakes. Leaving the museum, walk towards the administration building noting the gates emblazoned with the slogan *Arbeit macht frei* ('work sets you free').

Walking through the gates, you come to the roll call square. Looking directly ahead, you will see the large monument with the stone sculpture 'Liberation' designed by Rene Graetz.

To the left of the monument, you will note a grey structure, which is a protective covering for the camp crematoria. This area was known by the SS as 'Station Z' and was comprised of an execution and punishment area, a gas chamber, and four fixed ovens for the disposal of bodies. The area was intact at the time of the liberation of the camp. In 1952, it was blown up by members of the Militarised People's Police. Nine years later, the remains were recovered and partly reconstructed. A protective roof was installed by the museum authorities; this remained in place until structural deterioration led to its demolition in 2004. The current protective roof was installed shortly afterwards.

Opposite the execution trench, you will see several large photographs of Soviet prisoners. I always ask people on tours I am guiding to look into the eyes of each prisoner; the look of utter hopelessness on their faces speaks volumes about the terrible conditions prisoners endured and the countless atrocities committed in this camp.

The first Soviet prisoners arrived at the camp in August 1941. Within three months, some 11,000 Soviet prisoners were being held in the camp. Conditions were terrible, and mass executions steadily reduced their numbers. The most common method of execution was by shooting in the so-called 'Neck Shot Facility'. Here, an estimated 10,000 Soviet officers and men were murdered. Estimates of the total number of Soviet prisoners killed in the camp vary from 11,000 to 18,000.

Stalin's eldest son, Lieutenant Yakov Dzhugashvili, was held prisoner in Sachsenhausen following his capture at the Battle of Smolensk on 16 July 1941. Later, the German authorities offered to exchange him for Field Marshal Friedrich von Paulus who had been captured at Stalingrad. Stalin turned the offer down, stating that, 'I will not trade a marshal for a lieutenant.' On 14 April 1943, Dzhugashvili was shot and killed. Contemporary reports indicated that he had been shot while approaching the 'Neutral Zone', which bordered the electric fence. More recent reports show that he was shot for refusing to obey an order to return to his barracks. In March 1945, Stalin talked with Zhukov about his son; at this time, Stalin may not have known that he was already dead. He was certain that his son would not return home alive. Despite their strained relationship, Stalin's perception of a son he had once referred to as a 'mere cobbler' was perhaps softening a little. When the death of his son was confirmed, he rehabilitated him in the knowledge that he had died honourably.

Apart from being a place of terrible suffering, Sachsenhausen was also the setting for the largest counterfeiting operation in the history of economic warfare. Operation Bernhard was an audacious plot to destabilise the British economy by flooding it with fake currency. In 1942, Jewish prisoners began forging backdated £5, £10, £20, and £50 notes. Some nine million notes were produced in total, with a value of £134,000,000. In February 1945, the American dollar was finally perfected, but production at the site ceased before they could be produced in quantity. Large numbers of British fake notes remained in circulation for many years, prompting the Bank of England to withdraw all notes larger than £5. It was not until 1964 that the process of producing larger denomination notes began again.

The liberation of Sachsenhausen in April 1945 did not bring an end to the camp being used as a place of detention, torture, and execution. The former Special Camp built in 1940, consisting of brick built barracks was later used as a Soviet prison (Special Camp No. 7). The prisoners largely consisted of Soviet citizens, whom, after interrogation by SMERSH, had been deemed as 'Traitors to the Motherland.' German prisoners of war awaiting transport to Siberia were also held at the camp. The Soviet camp reached its full capacity of 12,000 prisoners by the end of 1945. The majority of prisoners were housed in the original wooden barracks. By 1946, the camp was seriously overcrowded as the prisoner population (which included 2,000 women) had swollen to some 16,000. In 1948,

Soviet propaganda from 1945: 'Destruction of Fascist nest forever'. (*Author's collection*)

Sachsenhausen clock showing the exact time of the liberation on 22 April 1945.

approximately 5,000 prisoners were granted an amnesty. The same year, the camp was re-designated as Special Camp No. 1. In early 1950, 5,500 prisoners were handed over to the East German authorities. The remaining prisoners were freed soon after. In the spring of 1950, the camp was finally shut down.

In 1995, the museum authorities expanded the memorial site to include Special Camp No. 7. Fifteen of the brick built barracks have been preserved, and there is an excellent museum on site that tells the story of the camp. An information leaflet, which is available describes conditions in the camp:

> Hunger and cold prevailed in the Special Camp. The inadequate hygienic and sanitary conditions and the insufficient nourishment led to disease and epidemics. Usually the barracks were overcrowded; the prisoners had to sleep on the bare wood frames until 1947, when the Soviet camp administration distributed blankets and bags of straw. The only clothing which the prisoners had during their imprisonment was what they were wearing at their time of arrest. The possession of personal items, particularly books and writing material was strictly forbidden. Violations of these rigid camp regulations, which were for the most part unknown to most of the prisoners, resulted in harsh punishment imposed by the Soviet guard personnel or the German prisoners who held special functions.

Several of the brick barrack buildings are open to visitors; inside, you can see recorded interviews on television monitors in which former prisoners describe the terrible conditions they were forced to endure. The visit to the memorial site is not an easy one as it can be physically and mentally exhausting. Like all sites of this nature, it is best to go prepared by doing some background reading beforehand.

History

It is thought that Albert the Bear (the first Margrave of Brandenburg) was responsible for founding Oranienburg by ordering the construction of a castle on the banks of the River Havel. However, it was not until forty-six years after the Margrave's death that the town was first officially mentioned in a document dating to 1216. At this time, the town was known as Botzow; it was not until 1653 that the name was changed following the construction of Schloss Oranienburg (a castle built in the Dutch style by Louise Henriette of Orange-Nassau, the wife of Friedrich Wilhelm I). Her son later extended and ornately decorated the castle, making it one of the most opulent in Germany.

Silvio Gessell (the founder of the 'Free Economy' movement) lived in the town between 1911 and 1915. He returned in 1927 and remained until his death three years later. Gesell's economics based upon the 'Three Fs' (free money, free land, and free trade) were practiced in the town until the National

Socialists came to power in 1933. Some of his followers were arrested and taken into 'protective custody' in the 'Wild Camp' set up by the Stormtroopers in Oranienburg. During the sixteen months in which the camp operated, approximately 3,000 people were imprisoned in primitive conditions. Some sixteen prisoners are known to have been murdered by sadistic guards.

During the war years, the town also played an important role in the German atomic programme. The Auer Company uranium processing plant provided material for nuclear experiments at the Kaiser Wilhelm Institute in Berlin. The plant was heavily bombed on 15 March 1945, resulting in the complete destruction of all of the above ground installations. Oranienburg was bombed thirteen times and it is thought that approximately 1,500 of the 10,000 bombs dropped on the town failed to detonate. A 2012 article in *Der Spiegel* estimated that the task of clearing all of the unexploded ordnance will take decades and will cost in excess of 400 million Euro.

16

End Game

Following Heinrici's dismissal, Colonel General Kurt Student was appointed as commander of what little remained of Army Group Vistula (though by this time, Army Group Elbe would have been a more accurate title). While the Army Group awaited his arrival, General Kurt von Tippelskirch assumed temporary command. Changes in the command structure at this stage were pointless as the headlong dash of fast-moving Soviet armoured columns rendered the establishment of effective German defence lines all but impossible.

The High Command issued orders for Army Group Vistula to hold the line in the Mecklenburg lake district. There were few natural barriers other than the lakes. Furthermore, no defensive positions had been prepared along a line that was simply too long for the limited forces available to defend. It was clear that dogged determination and combat skill were no longer enough to compensate for the overwhelming numerical superiority in men and machines enjoyed by the Red Army. Despite the impossibility of achieving any sort of favourable outcome, Colonel Eismann nonetheless praised the steadfastness and sheer professionalism of the troops who had held on for so long:

> There was absolutely nothing left to do but to retreat step by step towards the west. Both the 3rd Panzer Army as well as the 21st Army reported that their fighting potential was decreasing rapidly. There were gaps everywhere. A continuous front could no longer be formed. Thus, the Russians broke through our thin lines daily; it was only with much effort that our forces were able to withdraw and avoid being cut off and encircled by the enemy forces. One might believe that here it already looked like a general flight. This was not the case. Here and there one could observe some retreats which looked more like routs. In general, it must be said that the troops on the front managed to fight the enemy off, right up to the last, in spite of their superior forces...

Despite the orders given to hold the line, the Soviet breakthrough was as Eismann noted—something of a foregone conclusion. The breach in the German line was made by General Ivan Fedyuninski's 2nd Shock Army and Batov's 65th Army, taking the towns of Anklam and Greifswald in the course of their drive towards Stralsund.

Rokossovsky's push towards Lubeck gave Eismann cause for concern as there was a real possibility of Soviet forces positioning themselves between the remnants of the 3rd Panzer Army and the Western Allies. Unconfirmed reports received on 30 April suggested that Soviet forces had penetrated as far as Wismar. Thus, the defence of the sector between the Schwerin Lake and Wismar by elements of 3rd Panzer Army became vitally important with regard to maintaining an escape corridor to the west. The fighting was bitter, Eismann recalling that the 3rd Panzer Army, 'threw in everything that they could scrape together at the Russians in this area.' Of equal concern to Eismann was the growing gap between the 3rd Panzer Army and the 21st Army. Contact between the two forces had been lost, Eismann recalling that, 'The 3rd Panzer Army didn't have any contact with the 21st Army, nor did they know anything about their position.' The flank southwest of Rostock was effectivelly open.

Meanwhile, in Berlin itself, the so-called 'Race to the Reichstag' was won by Zhukov. The planting of the Red Banner by Sergeants Mikhail Yegorov and

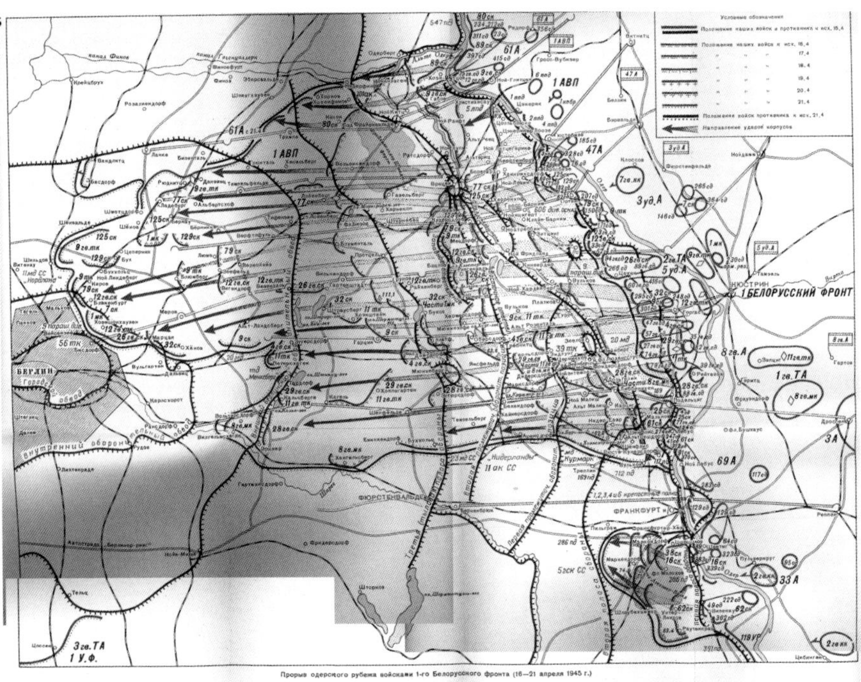

Soviet map showing the advance of the 1st Belorussian Front.

Meliton Kantaria on 30 April 1945 symbolised the defeat of Hitler's Germany. Moreover, Hitler had taken his own life in the bunker, thus making his divorce from the German people complete. Approximately three hours after Hitler's death, Grand Admiral Karl Dönitz was notified that Hitler had named him as his successor. Later that evening, Dönitz requested the presence of Keitel and Jodl at his headquarters in Plön in order to discuss the military and political situation. Keitel and Jodl set off the following morning, *en route* meeting with General Student at Wismar to brief him on his role. Confirmation of Hitler's death in Berlin finally reached Dönitz shortly after Keitel and Jodl's arrival during the early afternoon.

Dönitz's adjutant, Corvette Captain Walter Ludde-Neurath recorded his recollections of the subsequent meetings that took place between the new *Führer*, Keitel, Jodl, and Schwerin von Krosigk, who had accepted the title of Leading Minister in the new administration. As the deliberations of the new government had a direct bearing on the fate of Army Group Vistula, Ludde-Neurath's memories and impressions are worth noting in the following extract:

> From the moment Dönitz took office he saw his foremost task in ending the war as quickly as possible, in order to avoid further senseless bloodshed on both sides. There seemed to be two radically different possibilities. One was capitulation, the other a simple stopping of the fighting. The question whether the second solution was not perhaps the simpler and more honourable one was discussed at length. This point raised grave inner conflicts. The bitterness of unconditional surrender, and its shocking consequences, were known. However, after carefully weighing all factors, Dönitz decided in favour of an official surrender controlled from above. His reasons for this decision were that further loss of blood and property would be avoided, that chaos would be prevented, and that the victors would find themselves under some obligation, however vague.
>
> The question remained how such a surrender could be accomplished. Since Roosevelt's and Churchill's conference at Casablanca it was known that the Allies would accept nothing but unconditional surrender, extended simultaneously on all fronts. Such a surrender implied that all German troop movements should stop at once. Such a surrender was eliminated from the discussions immediately. It could not be carried out. The eastern armies would not have complied with it under any circumstances. The signature under a document embodying such terms would thereby be meaningless, and the new government would find itself unable to fulfil the obligations assumed by its very first official act.
>
> There remained only one possible course of action: the retreat of the eastern forces, together with as large a number of refugees as possible, to the demarcation line that was now known. This operation would require at

> least eight to ten days. During that time, the evacuation across the Baltic Sea from the Gulf of Danzig, from Courland, and from the pockets along the Pomeranian coast would be continued. Meantime, efforts would be made in the west to accomplish partial surrender.
>
> While these discussions went on, events hurried forward. Montgomery's rapid advance forced Dönitz to leave his present headquarters and move north to the town of Flensburg on the Danish border, to gain at least a few more days of freedom of action. Before leaving, he ordered the Hamburg Broadcasting Station to announce the news of Hitler's death to the nation... And later that night, Dönitz's own proclamation followed... This proclamation was Dönitz's program. It was addressed to the western powers even more than to the German people. It was his first statement—almost imploring in tone—of what he intended to do. Simultaneously with its publication, Dönitz authorised all units of Army Group Vistula to use every opportunity for separate surrender to the western powers. Next, he charged one of his most trusted naval officers, Admiral von Friedburg, to seek contact with Marshal Montgomery and attempt to accomplish a surrender of the armies in northern Germany to the western Allies.

The plan that emerged from the meetings was quickly translated into specific movement orders for Army Group Vistula. Now, there was a real chance that the remnants of the fighting forces in the east could be saved.

While the deliberations of the new Dönitz administration were taking place, Student had made his way to Army Group Vistula's headquarters at Schönwalde. Shortly after his arrival, the formal transfer of command from von Tippelskirch took place. The subsequent briefing by General Erich Dethleffsen was remembered by Eismann as being something of a farce:

> I was treated to one surprise after another. It was absolutely amazing how clear the situation appeared to be to our chief-of-staff. The obscure facts were all glossed over. General Student asked many questions, but seemed to be of the opinion, in spite of all his experiences of late, that the army group should go on the defensive between the Elbe, Lake Schwerin, and the coastline. The Americans in our rear weren't even discussed; they didn't seem to exist. I was rather surprised at the optimism of these three high dignitaries.

Like most new commanders, Student's initial assessment on taking over a battlefront was unjustifiably optimistic. However, his illusions were quickly shattered on the following day by Eismann's report detailing the final collapse of the Army Group. In the very short time in which Student exercised command, it is clear that his influence on operational matters was practically non-existent. Having experienced undue difficulties in maintaining contact with Student, the High Command contemplated replacing him with *Generalfeldmarschall* Ernst Busch. It no longer mattered who was in command, as the headquarters of Army Group Vistula ceased to function on 2 May. In all probability, Student and his staff were fleeing to safety in the west.

The disintegration of Army Group Vistula's headquarters coincided with orders from the High Command to move as many troops as possible behind a line running from Wismar–Schwerin–Ludwigslust–Domitz. From this new position, negotiations regarding local surrenders to British and American forces could be more easily facilitated. In reality, no such orders were needed. The narrow gap of just over 30 kilometres separating the Allied and Soviet forces meant that German commanders were now forced to act on their own initiative in order to secure safety for their remaining troops in the west.

One of the first commanders to make contact was General von Tippelskirch, who sent Colonel von Varnbuhler to act as his intermediary in a meeting with General 'Jumpin Jim' Gavin, commander of the American 82nd Airborne Division. Gavin declined von Varnbuhler's request for wounded soldiers and civilians to be allowed to pass through the American lines. He also declined a request that the 21st Army might be allowed to surrender to the Western Allies rather than the Soviets. However, after interrupting the discussions to confer with Montgomery's headquarters, Gavin let it be known that under certain conditions, a surrender to American or British forces might be possible. However, such an arrangement could only be made with the commanding officer of the 21st Army.

Time was of the essence, and so, without delay, von Tippelskirch set off for Gavin's headquarters located near Ludwigslust. The discussion centred upon the issue of surrender; von Tippelskirch argued that his troops would never voluntarily give themselves up to the Red Army:

> My troops, disciplined though they are, would not carry out my orders to give themselves up to the Russians. They do not fear to meet the Russians on the battlefield, but they fear the treatment they will receive in Russian prison camps. If I were to order surrender in the east, there would be an immediate chaotic mass flight to the west, with consequences you can easily imagine. The Russians would probably strike at my fleeing troops and start a slaughter amongst them and the civilians on every road ... I must be able to continue fighting against the Russians. I must be able to keep the Russians from piercing my lines, and give my troops the chance to move to the west without being scattered by the Russians. If that can be made possible, my troops will not fire a single shot in your direction, and they will drop their arms as soon as they meet your forces.

Gavin was left in something of a quandary by this request. On the one hand, he wished to give in to his humanitarian instincts; while on the other, he had to maintain his obligations to his Soviet allies. Von Tippelskirch wracked his brains for a solution, then he said:

> Couldn't we find a formulation that would make no mention of your Russian allies? If we could just confine ourselves to stating my obligation to have my troops drop their arms when they reach your lines?

Gavin then gave permission for von Tippelskirch to draft the following order to his troops:

> 21st Army will continue the withdrawal and will prevent Russian breakthroughs. Upon meeting American or British forces during the withdrawal, everybody will stop fighting, lay down arms, and deliver himself into their custody.

After making a few small amendments, Gavin passed on the order to Montgomery's headquarters. A reply was received after thirty minutes accepting the formulation. By dawn, the order had been distributed to the troops of the 21st Army. It was to prove their salvation.

The following morning, von Tippelskirch and 140,000 troops entered captivity with the Americans. It was not a minute too soon as the first Soviet tanks appeared before the American lines around noon. In order to speed up the passage of troops, the Americans screened and then separated civilians from the marching column. None of the civilians seeking shelter with the German troops were allowed to pass as the movement of troops from east to west had taken all morning.

Similar negotiations took place regarding the surrender of the 3rd Panzer Army, after which the bulk of von Manteuffel's forces surrendered to the British at Mecklenburg-Vorpommern. Manteuffel himself, together with a smaller number of troops were taken prisoner at Hagenow by the American 8th Armoured Division. General Steiner, who had refused to carry out Hitler's order to relieve Berlin, was taken prisoner at Golbosen on the Elbe on 3 May. South of Berlin, Wenck's rescue mission had saved what was left of Busse's forces from total destruction at the hands of the Soviets. General von Edelsheim negotiated the surrender of the 12th Army and the remnants of the 9th Army. The surrender was duly accepted by the American 9th Army at Stendal where the bulk of the German forces entered captivity. Some elements of the 9th and 12th Armies surrendered on American held territory on the Elbe on 5 May. General Wenck was taken prisoner as his troops crossed the Elbe at Angermünde two days later. General Busse, escaped captivity until 29 July when he was finally taken prisoner in his home town of Wallerstein.

APPENDIX I

Principal German Commanders

Colonel General Gotthard Heinrici

Gotthard Heinrici joined the Imperial German Army as a cadet in a Thuringian Infantry Regiment on 8 March 1905. After attending a course for basic officer training in Hannover, he was promoted to second lieutenant on 18 August 1906. After a spell as adjutant to the 2nd Battalion of his Regiment, he was promoted as first lieutenant on 17 February 1914. Following the outbreak of war in August 1914, Heinrici fought at Namur where he was awarded the Iron Cross 2nd Class on 27 September 1914. His unit was then transferred to the Eastern Front where he fought at the Masurian Lakes, Tannenberg, Łódz, and Rawka-Bzura. He was promoted to the rank of captain on 18 June 1915 and received the Iron Cross 1st Class the following month.

His unit was transferred back to the Western Front in September 1915. In May 1916, he was appointed adjutant of the 83rd Infantry Brigade, which was heavily engaged at Verdun. After receiving staff training, Heinrici served in numerous staff positions. He then undertook a general staff officer training course, which qualified him for his next appointment as adjutant with the 7th Army Corps in October 1917. In December, he was transferred to the 8th Army Corps where he held the same position. On 28 February 1918, Heinrici took up the position of operations officer with the 203rd Infantry Division. He was subsequently awarded the Prussian Knight's Cross of the Royal House of Hohenzollern.

In 1940, Heinrici commanded the 12th Corps of General Erwin von Witzleben's 1st Army. He then participated in the containment of the French Saar Offensive and German breakthrough of the Maginot Line. During Operation Barbarossa, he served in the 2nd Panzer Army under the command of Colonel General Heinz Guderian. He was given command of the 4th Panzer Army on 26 January 1942. His forces were heavily engaged in holding back Zhukov's counter-stroke outside of Moscow. Vastly outnumbered, his forces nonetheless held on for ten weeks. After receiving the Oak Leaves to his Knight's Cross in November 1943, he was relieved of his command on the grounds of ill health. In reality, Goering had him removed for his failure to destroy Smolensk in line with the scorched-earth policy.

After eight months of forced retirement, Heinrici was brought back to active service in Hungary as commander of the 1st Panzer Army and the 1st Hungarian Army. He succeeded in maintaining the integrity of his force as it retreated into Slovakia. For his achievements, he was awarded the Swords to the Oak Leaves of his Knight's Cross on 3 March 1945. On 20 March, he replaced Himmler as commander of Army Group Vistula. He was tasked with preventing the Soviets breaking out from their bridgeheads on the Oder. However, he was hampered by Hitler's conviction that the Red Army did not intend to thrust directly at Berlin. After conducting a brilliant defence on the Oder against overwhelming odds, he ordered a staggered withdrawal on his own initiative. Keitel subsequently relieved him of command, bringing to an end a forty-year military career.

After his dismissal, Heinrici headed north to join the Dönitz administration based in Plön. He was taken into British custody on 28 May 1945. He was held in a number of prison camps including the London District Cage. This was followed by a brief spell in America, where he underwent questioning on his operations against Soviet Forces. On 12 May 1948, he was transferred to Camp 186 in preparation for his repatriation, which took place nine days later. Following his release, he lived with his wife in Endersbach. Heinrici died aged eighty-four on 13 December 1971. His wife, Gertrude, survived him by ten years. It is of special note that his wife was half Jewish. Hitler personally protected his wife and two children from persecution by the issuance of a certificate declaring them to be of 'German blood.'

General Hasso von Manteuffel

Hasso von Manteuffel's military career began in 1908 when he enrolled at the Cadet Corps military school at Naumburg/Saale. Three years later, he entered the Senior Cadet Institute at Lichterfelde. Manteuffel joined the 5th Squadron of the 3rd Hussar Regiment on 22 February 1916. On 12 October, he was wounded by shrapnel in the right thigh near Bapaume. He returned to active duty in February 1917, after which he transferred to the general staff of the 6th Infantry Division. During November–December 1918, he was involved in protecting the bridge over the Rhine at Cologne from revolutionary elements. On 20 December 1918, he transferred to the Replacement Squadron of the 3rd Hussar Regiment. The following month, he was made adjutant of the *Freikorps* unit von Oven in Berlin.

Following the establishment of the 'Empire Defence' force (*Reichswehr*) in 1919, he transferred to the 25th Cavalry Regiment. He then became a squadron leader in the 3rd Prussian Mounted Regiment, following which he served for seven years as the regimental adjutant. On 15 October 1935, he was appointed to command the 2nd Motorcycle Rifle Battalion of the 2nd Panzer Division, commanded by General Heinz Guderian. Over the next four years, he became a tank specialist and instructor at Wünsdorf and later at Krampnitz, where he remained until 1941.

On 1 May 1941, Manteuffel was given the command of the 1st Battalion of the 7th Regiment of the 7th Panzer Division. He took part in Operation Barbarossa, his unit participating in the attack across the Memel river and subsequent capture of Vilnius. The division continued to advance eastwards through Minsk and Vitebsk before taking part in the capture of Smolensk in July 1941. The following month, he assumed command of the 6th Regiment after Colonel Erich von Unger was killed in action. In November, the 6th Regiment took part in the encirclement battle at Vyasma and later succeeded in capturing a bridge across the Volga-Moscow Canal. Following a period of dogged defence in the wake of Zhukov's counter offensive, the 7th Panzer Division was transferred to France in May 1942 for a much needed period of rest and rebuilding.

On 5 February 1943, Manteuffel was sent to Africa to command an *ad hoc* division consisting of the Luftwaffe Regiment *Barenthin,* the 160th Panzer Regiment, the 11th Parachute Pioneer Battalion, and the Italian 10th *Bersaglieri* Regiment. This division took part in Colonel General Hans Jurgen von Arnim's 'Operation Ox Head', a series of attacks designed to expand the Tunis bridgehead and create space for operational manoeuvre. The operation succeeded in pushing back the British, but was dismissed by *Generalfeldmarschall* Erwin Rommel as being 'a mere waste of strength.' On 31 March, Manteuffel was evacuated from Tunisia, suffering from illness and exhaustion. After a period of recuperation, he was promoted to the rank of major-general and took over the command of the 7th Panzer Division. Following its transfer to the Eastern Front, the 7th Panzer Division took part in fierce battles at Kharkiv, Belgorod, Akhtyrka, the Dnieper river, and Kiev. In late November, Manteuffel's troops recaptured Zhitomir.

On 1 February 1944, Manteuffel was appointed commander of the *Panzergrenadier* Division *Grossdeutschland.* The division fought in defensive battles west of Kirovograd. After executing a successful withdrawal across the Ukraine, Manteuffel took his division into Romania in late March 1944 where a series of defensive actions were fought at Lasy, Târgu Mureş, and Podu Iloaiei. The division then had a period of rest and refitting in Romania before beginning the transfer to East Prussia in late July. Heavy combat at Vilkaviškis in Lithuania resulted in considerable tank losses. The town was taken, only to be recaptured by the Red Army in August. Following his recall to Berlin, Manteuffel was promoted to general of Panzer troops on 1 September and given the command of the 5th Panzer Army for the forthcoming offensive through the Ardennes. Slated for a supporting role in the great offensive, the 5th Panzer Army went on to make the deepest penetrations into the American lines. Follwing the failure of the offensive, he was transferred back to the Eastern Front where he replaced Colonel General Erhard Raus as commander of the 3rd Panzer Army on 10 March 1945.

With great skill, Manteuffel held his extended front along the Oder until Marshal Rokossovsky's forces succeeded in establishing a bridgehead south of Stettin on 26 April. Following Colonel General Heinrici's dismissal, Manteuffel was offered the command of Army Group Vistula. He refused, citing his reason as Heinrici's unfair treatment at the hands of Field Marshal Keitel. On 3 May, Manteuffel surrendered his 3rd Panzer Army to British forces at Hagenow.

Following his release from captivity in December 1946, he entered politics and, from 1953 to 1957, was a member of the German Parliament as a representative of the Free Democratic Party. In 1965, he was involved in the publication of the unit history entitled *The 7th Panzer Division in the Second World War: Employment and combat of the Ghost Division 1939–1945.* Three years later, he lectured at the West Point Military Academy on winter warfare. In 1970, he co-authored *Alternative to Armageddon: The Peace Potential of Lightening War* with Colonel Wesley W. Yale and General Issac D. White. Manteuffel appeared in the acclaimed 1970s documentary series *World at War.* He died on 24 September 1978 while on holiday in the Tyrol.

APPENDIX II

Hitler's Order of the Day (15 April 1945)

Soldiers of the Eastern Front!

For the last time our deadly enemies, the Jewish Bolsheviks, have rallied their massive forces for an attack. They intend to destroy Germany and to exterminate the people. Many of you eastern soldiers know well the fate that threatens, above all, German women, girls, and children. While the old men and children will be murdered, the women and girls will be reduced to barrack-room whores. The remainder will be marched off to Siberia.

We have been expecting this attack, and since January have done everything possible to construct a strong front. The enemy will be greeted with massive artillery fire. Gaps in our infantry have been filled by countless new units. Our front is being strengthened by emergency units, newly raised units, and by the *Volkssturm.*

This time the Bolsheviks will meet the ancient fate of Asia, he must and shall bleed to death before the capital of the German Reich.

Whoever fails in his duty at this moment behaves as a traitor to our people. The regiment or division which abandons its position acts so disgracefully that they will be shamed by the women and children braving the terror of bombing in our cities.

Above all, be on your guard against the few treacherous officers and soldiers, who in order to preserve their pitiful lives, fight against us for Russian pay, perhaps even wearing German uniform. Anyone ordering you to retreat will, unless you know him personally, be immediately arrested and, if necessary, killed on the spot, no matter what rank he may hold.

If everyone on the Eastern Front does his duty in these coming days and weeks, the last assault of Asia will crumble, just as the invasion by our enemies in the west will fail in the end, in spite of everything.

Berlin remains German, Vienna will be German again, Europe will never be Russian.

Form yourselves into sworn brotherhoods to defend, not just the empty concept of a Fatherland, but your homes, your wives, your children, and, with them, our future.

In these hours, the whole German people looks to you, my eastern warriors, and only hope that by your resolution and fanaticism, thanks to your weapons, and under your leadership, the Bolshevik assault will be choked in a bath of blood. At this moment, in which fate has removed from the earth the greatest war criminal of all time, the turning point of this war will be decided.

Adolf Hitler

APPENDIX III

Principal Soviet Commanders

Marshal Georgy Zhukov

Georgy Zhukov was born into a peasant family in Strelkovka on 1 December 1896. His childhood was very hard, working first in the fields and then being apprenticed to a Moscow based furrier at the age of twelve. He completed his apprenticeship in 1912, after which he entered the fur business. However, his career was cut short following his conscription into the Army in August 1915. He served in the 189th Reserve Infantry Battalion of the 5th Reserve Cavalry Regiment. The following month, Zhukov was sent to the Ukraine for training with what would become the 10th Cavalry Division. In the spring of 1916, he was selected for non-commissioned officer training. In August, he returned to his unit, which was now designated as the 10th Dragoon Novgorod Regiment.

Zhukov's unit was deployed to the South-west Front, where it fought mainly as infantry in the wooded and mountainous Bystritsky region. The unit suffered large casualties, including Zhukov himself, who suffered concussion as a result of an exploding mine. Zhukov, who had been twice decorated with the Cross of St George for acts of bravery, including the capture of a German officer, was then assigned to a training command. On 28 February 1917, he was elected as chairman of the Squadron Soldier's Committee, which, in the incresingly Bolshevised Army, was responsible to the Regimental Soviet. Three months later, the Soviet made the decision to issue certificates of discharge to Zhukov's unit. He returned to Moscow following the seizure of power by the Bolsheviks in November 1917 and in February of the following year, he joined the Red Guards.

During the Civil War, Zhukov first served under the command of Semyen Mikhailovich Buddeny, who was to become a popular hero. Later, he served under the talented strategist Mikhail V. Frunze. In September 1919, he was wounded during the course of fierce hand-to-hand fighting between

Zaplavnoye and Akhtube. Following evacuation to hospital and recuperation leave, he was assigned to a cavalry school in Ryazan Province where he became a cadet master sergeant. In August 1920, Zhukov's battalion was deployed to Krasnodar, from where they attacked Pyotr Nikolayevich Wrangel's anti-Bolshevik White Army, which had consolidated in the Crimea and Black Sea area. The 9th Army (which included Zhukov's unit) was thrown against General Sergei Georgievich Ulagai's troops, which were threatening to join up with other anti-Bolshevik elements. In September, Ulagai's troops were thrown back. A peace treaty signed with the Poles on 12 October effectively ended Wrangel's resistance as without their assistance he was outnumbered by 4:1.

In May 1921, Zhukov's 14th Separate Cavalry Brigade was involved in hard fighting in Tambov Province against a peasant rebellion led by Alexander Antonov. The rebellion was put down without mercy, Tukhachevsky and Vladimir Antonov-Ovseyenko (People's Commissar of Military Affairs) signed an order, dated 12 June 1921, which read: 'The forests where the bandits are hiding are to be cleared by the use of poison gas. This must be carefully calculated, so that the layer of gas penetrates the forests and kills everyone hiding there.'

Subsequent publications in Communist newspapers later glorified the killing of 'bandits' with poison gas. Antonov was killed the following year. With the end of hostilities, Zhukov elected to remain in the Army. He was promoted to the post of Assistant Inspector of Cavalry in February 1931. Six years later, he was appointed as commander of the 3rd Cavalry Corps.

Zhukov survived the Great Purge largely because of Stalin's continued support of the Cavalry Corps. In early 1938, he was appointed as Deputy Commander of the Belorussian Military District. He was then selected to command the First Soviet-Mongolian Army Group against the Japanese Kwantung Army along the Mongolian-Manchurian border. On 20 August 1939, Zhukov launched his combined forces against the Japanese at Khalkhin–Gol. His fast moving tank columns first encircled and then annihilated the Japanese forces. The campaign ended on 15 September following the signing of a peace treaty. Zhukov was subsequently given the award Hero of the Soviet Union.

In 1940, the Main Military Council restored the ranks of general and admiral. Zhukov was promoted to the rank of General and was given command of the Kiev Special Military District. On 1 February 1941, he was appointed as chief of the general staff and in this capacity, subsequently took part in drawing up the strategic plans, which anticipated war against Germany and its allies. In the event, Stalin chose to ignore the elements of the plan, which called for a pre-emptive strike, instead adopting a policy of appeasement coupled with limited defensive preparations. Following the German attack on the Soviet Union on 22 June 1941, Zhukov was removed from his position on the General Staff. He was first appointed as commander of the Reserve Front and then as commander of the Leningrad Front. On 6 October, he was appointed as the *Stavka* representative for the Reserve and Western Fronts. In this capacity he oversaw defensive operations around Moscow and Rzhev.

In August 1942, Zhukov was appointed deputy commander-in-chief and dispatched to the South-western Front to coordinate operations around Stalingrad. In November, he was involved in coordinating the Kalinin and Western Fronts for the unsuccessful and costly Operation Mars. The official Soviet response to the operation was silence. However, a German 9th Army-report dated 15 December 1942 sheds some light on the debacle:

> The enemy leadership, which demonstrated skill and adaptability in the preparation and initial implementation of the offensive once again displayed its old weaknesses as the operation progressed. Indeed, the enemy has learned much, but he has again shown himself to be unable to exploit critically unfavourable situations. The picture repeats itself when operations which began with great intent and local successes degenerated into senseless, wild hammering at fixed front-line positions once they encounter initial heavy losses and unforeseen situations. This incomprehensible phenomenon appears again and again. But, even in extremis, the Russian is never logical; he falls back on his natural instinct, and the nature of the Russian is to use mass, steamroller tactics, and adherence to given objectives without regard to changing situations.

Despite the massive failure of the operation, Zhukov's reputation remained intact. Stalin needed him to contain the expected German summer offensive in 1943.

Zhukov was a *Stavka* coordinator during the great clash of arms at Kursk in July 1943. According to his memoirs, he met with Stalin, Vasilevsky and Antonov on 12 April to discuss the building up of Soviet forces in the threatened Kursk Salient. Marshal Rokossovsky later disputed Zhukov's role in the planning and execution of operations, later stating that, 'Comrades who had participated in the Kursk battle have come to me with questions. Why has Marshal Zhukov distorted history in his memoirs, claiming credit for things he never did? He shouldn't be permitted to do that.' General Nikolai Popel's denunciations of Zhukov were even more severe. In 1960, he wrote:

> The rudeness, which many commanders of my generation connected with the name of Marshal Zhukov, was not only his self-indulgence. His belief in his right to insult, to humiliate his subordinates, was transmitted like an infection. Martinet-like arrogance, which is alien to the truly democratic nature of our army, was adopted by some of the commanders, and at times even became their style.

Certainly, Zhukov could be extremely unpleasant with his subordinates at times. His egotism and Bonapartist tendencies were overlooked in Moscow as long as he continued to provide victories. On 31 July, the Presidium of the Supreme Soviet announced that Zhukov was to be awarded the Order of Suvorov (First Class) for his role in blunting the German Kursk offensive (Operation Citadel).

During 1944, Zhukov coordinated multi-front operations, most notably Operation Bagration, which resulted in the near complete destruction of the German Army Group Centre and the clearance of Belorussia and eastern Poland. The operation was characterised by the use of *maskirovka* (deception) and the concept of 'deep battle' developed by General Vladimr Triandafillov and Marshal Mikhail Tukhachevsky in the 1930s. On 12 November, Stalin made the decision to act as his own front coordinator, effectively demoting Zhukov to the command of 1st Belorussian Front. Zhukov was compensated by Stalin by being awarded the prize of Berlin. However, during the course of operations, Stalin initiated the so-called 'Race to the Reichstag' between Zhukov and Konev for the honour of taking the 'Lair of the Fascist Beast.' Zhukov won the race and, on 9 May, had the honour of accepting the German surrender at Karlshorst.

Following the German surrender, Zhukov acted as the first commander of the Soviet Occupation Zone. He briefly returned to Moscow in June to take a key role in the victory parade. Two months later, he participated in the Potsdam Conference. He did not know at the time that his career had peaked. In April 1946, he returned to Moscow fully expecting to be made Stalin's right hand man. Instead, his jealous and suspicious master had him hauled before the Higher Military Council on 1 June where he was accused of egoism and disrespect for his peers. Zhukov was been cut down to size because in Stalin's mind, his success and popularity made him a threat.

On 3 June 1946, Zhukov was stripped of his position of Commander-in-Chief of Soviet Ground Forces and transferred to the remote Odessa Military District to wither on the vine. In February 1948, he was transferred to the equally remote Urals Military District. On 4 March 1953, Zhukov received an unexpected recall to Moscow. Stalin was gravely ill and the party leadership led by Nikita Khrushchev wanted to appoint him as deputy minister of war. Zhukov accepted; his subsequent public rehabilitation began two months later when an article penned by him marking the eighth anniversary of victory over Germany was printed in *Pravda*. On 26 June, Zhukov took part in the arrest of Beria, who was subsequently tried and sentenced to death.

In January 1955, Zhukov was made minister of defence. His political career finally peaked the following year, after which disagreements with Khrushchev over the 'Open Skies' proposal soured their relationship. On 17 October 1957, Zhukov was denounced by the head of the armed forces political administration General A. S. Zheltov. Such a denunciation could only have been made with the active connivance of Khruschev. On 26 October, Zhukov was charged in person with egoism and Bonapartism. His second fall from grace came soon after when the Central Committee met on 28 October to ratify his forced retirement. After being forced from office, Zhukov maintained a low profile until Khruschev was deposed by Leonid Brezhnev in October 1964. On the twentieth anniversary of victory over Germany, Zhukov was given the honour of reviewing the military parade on Red Square. His memoirs were published five years later. By this time, Zhukov was dogged by ill health following a stroke. On 18 June 1974, he died after succumbing to a second stroke.

Marshal Ivan Stepanovich Konev

Ivan Stepanovich Konev was born into a peasant family from the Lodeyno District on 28 December 1897. He was raised by his father, as his mother had died during childbirth. Konev left school early to work in a timber mill. In 1916, he was conscripted into the Imperial Russian Army, serving first with the 2nd Heavy Artillery Brigade in Moscow and then the 2nd Separate Heavy Artillery Battalion on the South-western Front. In July 1917, he participated in the Kerensky Offensive as a non-commissioned officer. He was demobilised in December 1917 following the Russian Revolution.

Following his return home, Konev was elected as county military commissioner in the town of Nikolsk. During the Civil War, he was actively involved in the campaigns in the far eastern provinces of Russia against the forces of Admiral Alexander Kolchak and his successor Ataman Grigory Semyonov. In March 1921, he took part in the suppression of the Kronstadt Rebellion. After the Civil War, he completed a course for higher command personnel at the Frunze Academy. His subsequent rise to power was incredible. In July 1938, he was appointed as commander of the Far East-based 2nd Army. Two years later, he was given command of the Trans-Baikal Military District. The following year, he commanded the North Caucasus Military Distict. By this time, his political career was also flourishing as he had been elected as a delegate to the Supreme Soviet.

Following the German invasion in June 1941, Konev was given command of the 19th Army in the Vitebsk region. He successfully extricated his forces from the German pincers at Smolensk, an action which did not go unnoticed and led to his promotion to the rank of colonel general and command of the Western Front. An operation to clear up a German penetration led to disaster at Vyazma when a considerable portion of the Western Front and Reserve Front forces were surrounded. The causes of the catastrophe were investigated by the National Defence Commission. Zhukov was ordered by Stalin to take over command of the Western Front. Zhukov agreed, but successfully argued for the retention of Konev as deputy commander with additional responsibilities for the forces based around Kalinin.

Thanks to Zhukov, Konev survived and went on to command the Kalinin Front and then the Western Front for a second time during the fighting around Rzhev-Sychevskaya and Zhizdrinskaya. However, he was later removed from command after his forces suffered more than 290,000 casualties. Given another chance to prove himself, he was then given command of the Steppe Front, which participated in the repulse of the German attack at Kursk in July 1943. Konev's forces then took part in the liberation of Belgorod and Kharkov. In October, the Steppe Front was re-designated as the 2nd Ukrainian Front. In January 1944, Konev's forces participated in the Korsun-Shevchenovsky Offensive, which was notable for the successful employment of the doctrine of 'Deep Battle.' Although the operation did not lead to the complete collapse of the German front, significant damage was inflicted on six German divisions trapped in the Cherkassy–Korsun Pocket. For his part in the operation, Konev was rewarded with promotion to the rank of Marshal of the Soviet Union.

In May 1944, Konev was appointed as commander of 1st Ukrainian Front. His forces achieved success during the Lvov–Sandomierz Operation, creating a bridgehead on the left bank of the River Vistula. For his achievements, he was subsequently awarded the Order of Lenin and was made a Hero of the Soviet Union. In January 1945, his forces captured the important industrial region of Silesia. He then participated in the Oder-Berlin Operation, striking an important blow to the south of the city, which isolated the German forces of Army Group Centre. On 1 June, Konev became a Hero of the Soviet Union for the second time.

After the war, Konev's star remained in the ascendant. He replaced Zhukov as commander of Soviet Ground Forces and first deputy minister of Defence in 1946. He held these posts until 1950, when Stalin decided to cut him back down to size by transferring him to the command of the Carpathian Military District. Konev returned to prominence following Stalin's death, becoming a key ally of Nikita Khrushchev. In 1956, he was named as Commander-in-Chief of the Armed Forces of the Warsaw Pact. In 1960, Konev retired from active service. He briefly came out of retirement to command the Soviet forces in East Germany, after which he held the ceremonial post of inspector general of the Defence Ministry. In 1969, Konev's memoirs were published. He died three years later. His legacy is that of a highly educated, resourceful, but ruthless commander.

Marshal Konstantin Rokossovsky

Konstantin Rokossovsky was born in the small Russian town of Velikiye Luki on 21 December 1896. His father was of Polish origin, while his mother came from Belorussia. Shortly after his birth, the family moved to Warsaw following his father's appointment as a railway official. Five years later, his father was killed in a work related railway accident. In 1911, his mother died, leaving him and his younger sister Helena as orphans. Rokossovsky kept the family together by working as a labourer and then as a stonemason. In 1914, he was conscripted into the Imperial Russian Army. He served with distinction in the 5th Kargopol Dragoon Regiment. Having been wounded twice in actions in which he displayed outstanding courage, he was awarded the Cross of St George. Following the Russian Revolution, he joined the Communist Party and entered into service with the Red Army. In 1919, Rokossovsky took part in operations against Kolchak's 'White Guardsmen' in the Urals. He was wounded in the shoulder, but still succeeded in overrunning the enemy headquarters and killing their commander. For his courageous actions, Rokossovsky was awarded the prestigious Order of the Red Banner.

After attending the Frunze Military Academy, Rokossovsky served as an instructor in the Mongolian Army. In August 1937, he was caught up in the 'Great Purge' after being accused of having connections with the Polish and Japanese secret services. He spent the next three years as a prisoner in the notorious Kresty prison in Leningrad. During this time, he was tortured and forced to endure mock executions. On 22 March 1940, Rokossovsky was released and rehabilitated due to the shortage of experienced officers. He was given the rank of Colonel in the 5th Cavalry Corps. After participating in the occupation of Bessarabia, he was promoted to the rank of major-general and given command of the 9th Mechanised Corps. On the outbreak of hostilities with Germany on 22 June 1941, the 9th Mechanised Corps was deployed on the Southwestern Front under the overall command of Colonel General Mikhail Kirponos. Rokossovsky's unit participated in a Soviet offensive in the Lutsk-Dubno-Brody triangle. Stiff German resistance led to Kirponos calling off the offensive, an order which was immediately countermanded by Zhukov who insisted that the offensive continue at any cost. In a remarkable act of bravery by a recently rehabilitated traitor, Rokossovsky refused to carry out Zhukov's instructions, later stating in his memoirs:

> We had once again received an order to counterattack. However, the enemy outnumbered us to such a degree, that I took on the personal responsibility of ordering to halt the counteroffensive and to meet the enemy in prepared defences.

Rokossovsky's brave stand paid off as his forces stopped the advance of the German 14th Panzer Division in its tracks. Therefore, instead of being censured, he was promoted to his previous rank of lieutenant general and given the task of defending the bridgehead on the Vop river, which was threatened by the advance of the German 7th Panzer Division.

In the ensuing see-saw battle for Smolensk, Rokossovsky's forces played a key role in slowing down the German advance and holding the Yartsevo Corridor open long enough for substantial numbers of 16th Army troops to escape encirclement and destruction. After extricating his troops, Rokossovsky was given the difficult task of defending the Volokolamsk area situated to the north-west of Moscow. Despite a lack of troops and transportation, he succeeded in holding an unbroken line of defence. For his gifted leadership in the defence of Moscow, he was awarded the Order of Lenin. In March 1942, he was wounded by a shell splinter and subsequently spent two months recovering in a Moscow hospital. After being declared fit for duty, he again took up the command of the 16th Army. On 13 July, he was given his first operational command when Stalin named him as commander of the Bryansk Front. Two months later, he was given command of the Don Front, which took part in Operation Uranus. For his contribution in destroying the German 6th Army at Stalingrad, Rokossovsky was awarded the Order of Suvorov.

Stalin began to take note of Rokossovsky's achievements. His political rehabilitation was completed with the first of a series of important assignments in February 1943. In a diary entry from this time, Rokossovsky wrote, 'I'm appointed commander of the Central Front. It means Stalin has entrusted me to play the key part in the summer Kursk campaign.' Stalin's trust was not misplaced as Rokossovsky's Central Front successfully blunted Model's assault against the northern face of the Kursk Salient in July. Arguably his greatest achievement came the following year when he commanded 1st Belorussian Front during Operation Bagration. Rokossovsky distinguished himself by displaying a creative approach to operational thinking, which further impressed Stalin. This enormous offensive displayed the maturation of Soviet operational art and resulted in a crushing defeat upon the opposing forces of Army Group Centre. Rokossovsky was rewarded by promotion to the rank of marshal of the Soviet Union.

In November, Rokossovsky took over the command of the 2nd Belorussian Front, which fought bloody campaigns in East Prussia and Pomerania during the final months of the war. Denied the prize of Berlin, his forces went on to meet with the British 2nd Army at Wismar on 3 May 1945. On 24 June 1945, he had the honour of commanding the victory parade in Moscow (Zhukov was given the role of parade inspector). Stalin next tasked Rokossovsky with reorganising the Polish Army. In October 1949, he was appointed minister of national defence and marshal of Poland. Three years later, he was named as deputy chairman of the Council of Ministers. In 1956, a crowd of approximately 100,000 people gathered in Poznan to protest against harsh working conditions and their poor standard of living. The protests were brutally suppressed by Rokossovsky who sent in 10,000 troops and 400 tanks. The death of between seventy and 100 protesters prompted Moscow to introduce reforms. The subsequent rehabilitation of the activist and reformer Władysław Gómulka led to Rokossovsky being recalled to Moscow after the so-called 'Polish October.' This transitional period saw the hard-line Stalinist faction in Poland lose influence as the reformers faction led by Gómulka took control with Moscow's blessing. Rokossovsky summed up his own position by saying, 'In Russia, they say I'm a Pole, in Poland they call me Russian.' It would be true to say that he was never fully accepted by either.

Following his return to Moscow, Rokossovsky's former Soviet ranks and titles were restored. In July 1957, Khrushchev appointed him deputy minister of Defence and commander of the Transcaucasian Military District. The following year, Rokossovsky was appointed as chief inspector of the Ministry of Defence. He held this post until April 1962 when Khrushchev removed him from office for refusing to write an article condemning Stalin. In December 1966, he participated in carrying the remains of the Unknown Soldier to the Alexander Garden. Two years later, he succumbed to prostate cancer.

Lieutenant General Vasily Chuikov

Vasily Chuikov was born on 12 February 1900 to a peasant family in the village of Serebryanye Prudy. He left school at the age of twelve to work in a factory in St Petersburg. Following service alongside his brothers in the Russian Civil War, Chuikov joined the Communist Party and quickly earned promotion as a regimental commander. In 1925, he graduated from the Frunze Military Academy. After taking part in the invasion of Poland and the Winter War against the Finns, Chuikov was sent to China to act as a military advisor. Following Japan's invasion of China in 1937, Chuikov returned with a group of Army and Air Force officers to give support and guidance to Nationalist China's struggle against the invaders.

Chuikov was recalled to the Soviet Union in early 1942 as a result of the desperate need for experienced officers. He was given the command of Red Army forces in the city of Stalingrad. On being given the command, he reportedly said, 'We shall hold the city or die there.' The battle for the city raged for more than five months and ended with the destruction of the German 6th Army. Chuikov later talked about the epic battle with United Press reporter Henry Shapiro:

> Hitler put the best he had against Stalingrad. He did not spare quantity or quality. It was a battle for life or death. We were continuously attacked by great masses of infantry, tanks, artillery and planes. Our forces were not equal. The enemy had superiority at all points all the time.

Stalingrad was a major psychological turning point in the war. It was also a key part in the Red Army's difficult and painful regeneration as an effective fighting force.

After the victory at Stalingrad, Chuikov's 62nd Army was re-designated as the 8th Guards Army. Chuikov led his forces in campaigns in the Donets Basin, the Crimea and Belorussia. As part of the 1st Belorussian Front, the 8th Guards Army cut a swathe through Poland, before spearheading Zhukov's drive towards Berlin. On 2 May 1945, Chuikov accepted the surrender of German forces in Berlin. From 1949 until 1953, he served as commander-in-chief of Soviet forces in Germany. Two years later, he was elevated to the rank of marshal of the Soviet Union. In 1960, Chuikov was given command of the Soviet Union's ground forces. He held this important post for four years, after which he served as chief of civil defence. After taking up this appointment, he declared, 'If anyone attacks us again there will be a new Stalingrad, but this Stalingrad will be far away, somewhere in the West.' Chuikov remained in this post until his retirement in 1972. Ten years later, he died in Moscow aged eighty-two.

APPENDIX IV

Soviet Operational Art

German defensive doctrine and preparations for holding the approaches to Berlin against the anticipated Soviet assault in April 1945 have been well documented in a variety of publications over the years. Stephen Hamilton's recent two-volume history of Army Group Vistula provides an in-depth study of the German defences along the *Oderfront*. Popular histories such as Anthony Beevor's *Berlin*: *The Downfall 1945* and Cornelius Ryan's *Berlin 1945*: *The Last Battle* provide the reader with an accessible account of the last desperate attempts to hold off the rampaging Red Army. Soviet operations during this period have been given far less attention, particularly those based on the concept of 'Deep Battle'. Therefore, the following section will serve to acquaint the reader more fully with Soviet operational art and the development of deep mechanised operations.

With the increasing industrialisation of war, the problems of combat mass and mobility became more complex. The maturation of the tank concept greatly increased the scale of the battlefield, as fast moving, deep penetrations into enemy territory were now possible. The driving force behind the Soviet mechanisation of deep operations was Marshal Mikhail Tukhachevsky, who produced a master plan for the modernisation of the Red Army in 1927, only to have it rejected by Stalin. However, three years later, Stalin relented after he began to associate the onset of the Great Depression with a rising threat against the Soviet Union. Tukhachevsky was subsequently given permission to conduct a series of experiments based around the concepts of combined-arms units and so-called 'self-propelled combat means', which involved greater use of tanks, self-propelled artillery and armoured cars.

Tukhachevsky's radical reforms had the backing of Kliment Voroshilov, who in his capacity of People's Commissar for Defence of the Soviet Union argued that mechanisation would bring about a change in the future conduct of wars, one in which rapid advances into enemy territory promised the possibility of a short, decisive conflict. In 1931, Tukhachevsky became the Deputy Commissar of Military and Naval Affairs and Director of Armaments. Four years later, he was promoted to the rank of Marshal. With the greater authority that came with his rank, Tukhachevsky argued that war with Germany was inevitable, but could be won by delivering a series of lightning blows deep into the enemy flanks by powerful tank and combined-arms forces. His views were taken seriously and as such he was given the scope to further develop the modernisation and mechanisation of the Red Army.

Rapid Soviet industrialisation had created the means to turn Tukhachevsky's ideas into reality. However, Stalin's paranoia was fed by a series of plots and counterplots, which led to Tukhachevsky's downfall and the start of the 'Great Purge'. Reinhard Heydrich, the young and ambitious head of Himmler's security services was aware that Stalin was jealous of his more talented subordinates and wished to discredit them. A plot was hatched involving the forgery of incriminating letters that linked Tukhachevsky to the German secret services. Andre Brissaud, author of the book *The Nazi Secret Service* described how the Tukhachevsky dossier concocted by Heydrich fell into Stalin's greedy hands:

> A German emigre who lived in Prague and worked under the orders of S.S. Colonel Bohme put the last [*sic*] in touch with a friend and confidant of Dr Benes to whom he confided that a certain Alfred Naujocks in Berlin was ready to sell the Soviets a dossier which would destroy Marshal Tukhachevsky. President Benes, already alerted to the scent, fell into the new trap and told Stalin in a personal letter. The response from the Kremlin was immediate. Two of Iezhov's agents came to Prague, made contact with Bohme and went to Berlin where Naujocks, forewarned, awaited them. Three million gold roubles in banknotes and the Tukhachevsky dossier changed hands.

When the dossier was presented to Voroshilov, the military establishment promptly turned against Tukhachevsky, denouncing him as a traitor. Tukhachevsky was arrested on 22 May 1937. After undergoing torture, he signed a confession stating that he had been recruited as a German spy by Avel Enukidze. The blood splattered signed confession is still in the Moscow archives. Analysis of the blood splash pattern suggests that Tukhachevsky had received a blow to the head just before he signed.

Armed with a false confession extorted by extreme violence, Stalin's chief prosecutor Andrey Vyshinsky arranged for a show trial to be held. In a parody of justice, the special military tribunal reached a guilty verdict on 11 June. Tukhachevsky was executed at dawn the following day. The execution of Tukhachevsky opened the floodgates for a wave of denunciations and executions, which decapitated the higher echelons of the Red Army. By 1941, all that was left was a theory, but no acknowledged authors who could put it into practice. The harsh realities of war following Operation Barbarossa forced the Red Army to accept that radical change was needed. Slow, and in many ways painful reforms, finally created a force structure, which could carry out the deep operations envisaged by Tukhachevsky. By 1944, the Red Army had evolved to the point at which mobile operations achieved the goals set out in pre-war doctrine.

In 1956, Khrushchev denounced Stalin's purges at the twentieth Party Congress. However, it took some time for Tukhachevsky to be fully rehabilitated by the state. In 1963, the publication of A. I. Todorsky's biography signalled the real start of the process. Six years later, N. I. Koritsky's 1969 biography completed Tukhachevsky's political rehabilitation. Looking back on the dark period of the purges, Khrushchev lamented the loss of the Soviet Union's greatest theorist:

> I had known Tukhachevsky slightly and used to meet with him when I worked as First Secretary of the Moscow City and Regional communities. We used to talk on the telephone and see each other at plenums. He occasionally took me out into the field to show me some new weapon or new piece of engineering equipment. He had a deep understanding of military innovations and a high regard for them. I'm convinced that if he hadn't been executed, our army would have been much better trained and better equipped when Hitler attacked.

Khrushchev's lament is fairly typical of a school of thought, which emerged following Tukhachevsky's rehabilitation. The argument put forward was that the Soviet Union's calamitous combat experiences in the Winter War against the Finns and those following Operation Barbarossa could have been avoided if Tukhachevsky's doctrines had been followed. Alternative history has its place, but in this case serves to downplay the very real contributions Tukhachevsky made towards the final Soviet victory. Even if no one dared speak his name, Soviet commanders further developed his ideas into war winning manoeuvres at Stalingrad, Kursk and the approaches to Berlin. Only after Stalin's death and subsequent rehabilitation by Khruschev could the roots of victory in the Great Patriotic War be traced back to the genius of Tukhachevsky.

Bibliography

Applebaum, A., *Gulag: A History* (Penguin, 2004)

Beevor, A., *Berlin: The Downfall 1945* (Penguin, 2007)

Beevor, A., *The Second World War: 6 Years. 60 Million Lives Lost. No Human Life Untouched* (W&N, 2014)

Bahn, K., *Berlin 1945: The Final Reckoning* (Amber Books Ltd, 2004)

Bellamy, C., *Absolute War: Soviet Russia in the Second World War* (Macmillan, 2007)

Bessel, R., *Germany 1945: From War to Peace* (Simon and Schuster, 2012)

Bessel, R., *No Man's Land of Violence: Extreme Wars in the 20th Century* (Wallstein Verlag, 2006)

Boldt, G., *Hitler's Last Days: An Eye Witness Account* (Pen & Sword, 2006)

Brissaud, A., *The Nazi Secret Service* (Corgi, 1975)

Bullock. A., *Hitler and Stalin: Parallel Lives* (Fontana Press, 1998)

Chaney, O. P., *Zhukov* (David & Charles, 1972)

Chant, C., *Warfare and the Third Reich: The Rise and Fall of Hitler's Armed Forces* (Pavillion Books, 2015)

Chuikov, V. I., *The Fall of Berlin: With the Russian Army in Berlin—The Last Battle of Nazi Germany* (Ballantine Books, 1967)

Clark, A., *Barbarossa: The Russian-German Conflict 1941–45* (Weidenfeld & Nicholson, 1995)

Denny, I., *The Fall of Hitler's Fortress City* (Casemate Publishers, 2009)

Dobbs, M., *Six Months in 1945: FDR, Stalin, Churchill, and Truman: From World War to Cold War* (Random House, 2013)

Dupy, T. N., *The Value of Field Fortifications in Modern Warfare Volume 1* (Defence Nuclear Agency, 1979)

Duffy, C., *Red Storm on the Reich* (Routledge, 2014)

Erickson, J., *The Road to Berlin: Stalin's War with Germany Vol 2* (W&N, 2003)

Erickson, J., *The Soviet High Command: A Military-Political History, 1919–1941* (Routledge, 2006)

Fest, J. C., *Hitler* (Penguin Books, 1973)

Foley, C., *Commando Extraordinary: Otto Skorzeny* (Cassell, 1987)

Forczyk, R., *Georgy Zhukov* (Osprey Publishing, 2012)

Glantz, D. M., and House, J., *When Titans Clashed: How the Red Army Stopped Hitler* (University Press of Kansas, 1995)

Granahan, W. J., *The Fall and Rise of Marshal Tukhachevsky* (Parameters, Journal of the US Army War College, 1978)

Hamilton, A. S., *The Oder Front 1945: Generaloberst Gotthard Heinrici, Heersgruppe Weichel and Germany's Final Defence in the East, 20 March–3 May* (Helion & Company Ltd, 2011)

Hamilton, A. S., *The Oder Front 1945 Volume 2: Documents, Reports and Personal Accounts* (Helion & Company Ltd, 2014)

Hastings, M., *Armageddon: The Battle for Germany 1944–45* (Pan Books, 2004)

Keegan, J., *The Second World War* (Pimlico, 1989)

Kershaw, I., *Hitler: 1936–1945 Nemesis* (Penguin, 2001)

Kershaw, I., *The End: Germany 1944–45* (Penguin, 2012)

Kershaw, I., *The Hitler Myth: Image and Reality in the Third Reich* (Oxford University Press, 2001)

Kuby, E., *The Russians and Berlin, 1945* (Hill and Wang, 1968)

Le Tissier, T., *The Battle of Berlin 1945* (St Martin's Press, 1988)

Le Tissier, T., *The Siege of Kustrin 1945: Gateway to Berlin* (Pen & Sword, 2009)

Le Tissier, T., *Soviet Conquest: Berlin 1945* (Pen & Sword, 2014)

Le Tissier, T., *Zhukov at the Oder: The Decisive Battle for Berlin* (Praeger Publishers Inc, 1996)

Maudsley, E., *Thunder in the East: The Nazi-Soviet War 1941–1945* (Bloomsbury Academic, 2007)

Mcateer, S. M., *500 Days: The War in Eastern Europe 1944–1945* (Dorrance Publishing, 2009)

Merridale, C., *Ivan's War: The Red Army 1939–45* (Faber & Faber, 2005)

Minert, R. P., *In Harms Way: East German Latter-Day Saints in World War II* (Religious Studies Centre, Brigham Young University, 2009)

Miranda, J., *The Race to the Reichstag: The Battle of Berlin 1945* (World at War Magazine, 2012)

Montefiore, S. S., *Stalin: The Court of the Red Tsar* (W&N, 2014)

Naveh, S., *In Pursuit of Military Excellence: The Evolution of Operational Theory* (Routledge, 2013)

Overy, R., *Russia's War* (Penguin, 2010)

Overy, R., *The Dictators: Hitler's Germany and Stalin's Russia* (Penguin, 2005)

Overy, R., *The Third Reich: A Chronicle* (Quercus, 2011)
Read, A., and Fisher, D., *The Fall of Berlin* (Pimlico, 2002)
Roberts, G., *Stalin's General: The Life of Georgy Zhukov* (Icon Books Ltd, 2013)
Ryan, C., *Berlin 1945: The Last Battle* (New English Library, 1966)
Seaton, A., *The Russo-German War 1941–45* (Presidio, 1971)
Shirer, W., *The Rise and Fall of the Third Reich* (Arrow, 1991)
Sider, G. M., and Smit, G. A., *Between History and Histories: The Making of Silences and Commemorations* (University of Toronto Press, 1997)
Slowe, P., and Woods, R., *Battlefield Berlin: Siege, Surrender & Occupation, 1945* (Robert Hale, 1988)
Spahr, W. J., *Zhukov: The Rise & Fall of a Great Captain* (Presidio, 1993)
Thorwald, J., *Defeat in the East* (Bantam Books, 1980)
Toland, J., *The Last 100 Days* (Mayflower, 1968)
Tully, A., *Berlin: The Story of a Battle*: (eNet Press, 1963)
Williamson, G., *The Waffen SS (2): 6 to 10 Divisions* (Osprey Publishing, 2012)
Zhukov, G., *Marshal of Victory: The Autobiography of General Georgy Zhukov* (Pen & Sword, 2014)
Ziemke, E. F., *From Stalingrad to Berlin: Operation of Soviet Troops and the Wehrmacht. 1942–1945* (Tsentpoligraf, 2010)